Blood Ties Forever
The Re-Covering of the True Church

Dr. Royce L. Woods, Author

Trafford Publishing
1663 Liberty Drive, Suite 200
Bloomington, IN 47403

Order this book online at www.trafford.com
or email orders@trafford.com

Most Trafford titles are also available at major online book retailers.

Cover illustration by Stacy Alleyne

Printed in Victoria, BC, Canada.

ISBN: 978-1-4269-1906-0 (sc)
ISBN: 978-1-4269-1907-7 (dj)

Library of Congress Control Number: 2009937377

*Our mission is to efficiently provide the world's finest, most comprehensive book publishing
service, enabling every author to experience success. To find out how to publish your book,
your way, and have it available worldwide, visit us online at www.trafford.com*

Trafford rev. 1/6/10

www.trafford.com

North America & international
toll-free: 1 888 232 4444 (USA & Canada)
phone: 250 383 6864 ♦ fax: 812 355 4082

Blood Ties Forever

"And the Lord answered me, and said, write the vision, and make it plain upon tables, that he may run that readeth it. For the vision is yet for an appointed time, but at the end it shall speak, and not lie: though it tarry, wait for it; because it will surely come, it will not tarry."

Habakkuk 2:2-3 KJV

"The Lord God which gathereth the outcasts of Israel saith, yet will I gather others to him, beside those that are gathered unto him."

Isaiah 56:8 KJV

TABLE OF CONTENTS

Dedication

To my loving parents John and Mary Woods whose contributions to this work goes without saying. The unselfish love they shared with us during our formative years, is unsurpassed by any challenge I have encountered in my life.

Acknowledgements

My heartfelt thanks go to my wife Catherine, my daughter Aarin, to Virginia Hursey, Judy Mays, and all of you whose prayers and genuine support made this work possible.

All Glory, Honor, and Praise
Belongs to the
ONE
True and Living God
Who is the creator of both
Heaven and Earth

Through Him and Him alone
Have we received two **infallible** proofs;
An *idea* and a solution . . .
The idea is LOVE
The solution is BLOOD

Without LOVE there is only
Sorrow, sickness, suffering, & pain
And without BLOOD . . .
There is no life; only death

With His LOVE,
God had validated us;
And with His BLOOD
He has . . .

Vindicated us.

Dr. R. L. Woods

"God is up to something new. It's bigger than Messianic Judaism. It's bigger than Gentile Christianity. Both have been used mightily by God, but this new move will not look like a traditional synagogue, a traditional Church, or even a Messianic Synagogue, although it will have aspects of each. It will not be the one man show, but the one new man. It is Jewish and Gentile believers holding the baton together. The two have been made one in Jesus."

Sid Roth
The Race to Save the World

"So we are in a time of mutual awakening and a time of mutual activation. It is a time to make a stand, and a time to move out and win new territory."

"Task lie before us. Whether we are Jewish or Gentile, it is time to pray and proclaim, to give and receive. For some of us, it is time to take radical action. "

"God promises help, prosperity and provision to those who formally set themselves against His name and His people. Of course, for everyone a choice is involved. Everybody can choose to accept the offer or not. Those who accept will have a front-row seat as the final drama unfolds."

James W. Goll
The Coming Israel Awakening

Preface

"Unto the angel of the Church of Ephesus write; These things saith he that holdeth the seven stars in his right hand, who walketh in the midst of the seven golden candlesticks; I know thy works, and thy labour, and thy patience, and how thou canst not bear them which are evil: and thou hast tried them which say they are apostles, and are not, and hast found them liars: And hast borne, and hast patience, and for my name's sake hast laboured, and hast not fainted. Nevertheless I have somewhat against thee, because thou hast left thy first love. Remember therefore from whence thou art fallen, and repent, and do the first works; or else I will come unto thee quickly, and will remove thy candlestick out of his place, except thou repent. But this thou hast, that thou hatest the deeds of the Nicolaitanes, which I also hate. He that hath an ear, let him hear what the Spirit saith unto the Churches; To him that overcometh will I give to eat of the tree of life, which is in the midst of the paradise of God."

Revelation 2:1-7 KJV

Imagine living in a world where miracles and multiplied blessings are common place; where the kind of optimism that love and caring produces become the order of the day. This is the fruit of the candlestick which houses the anointed Spirit of God. For this reason, without the presence of the candlestick, the dynamics that are currently at play in the earth, such as global warming, unchecked viruses, financial collapse, moral decay, and man's continued inhumanity against his fellow man, will continue to go unabated and unaltered. That's why we are calling for the true Church to invoke the presence of God with an even greater sense of urgency.

This book was written purely from a Christian perspective. Therefore its intent is not to criticize any group of people, or advocate the dismantling or disavowing of any Christian organization. Our emphasis here is to analyze this amazing historical idea, in order to better present a God give solution. As Christians we seek counsel from a higher power, one who we believe has the profound ability to create, plan, direct and alter global events. However, in order for His plan to manifest itself, we must first be willing to return to Him that which He has created for His own purpose – as the Bible says - "His good pleasure". Luke 12:32

"And when they were come to Jerusalem, they were received of the Church, and of the apostles and elders, and they declared all things that God had done with them."
                                                            Acts 15:4 KJV

In the Book of Acts we have been formally introduced to the existence and the internal working of the Jerusalem Council. This penetrating knowledge creates the springboard from which our campaign has been launched; *the reestablishment of the Council in Jerusalem.*

"Blood Ties Forever" explores the Church's need for reconciliation with the Jewish nation, and also to develop a meaningful respect for the different ethnic groups referred to in scripture as the "remnant". This remnant is made up of those who God will use to introduce to the world at large this astonishing likeness of His divine design. This literary movement sets forth a well documented account of the distinct history of a unique people. The Church is being asked to vigorously pray for and support Israel, but many lack and are in need of a better understanding of these people, and God's apparent obsession with them. We

ask that you join our efforts to reconcile this prolonged and un-acceptable condition.

"And all things are of God, who hath reconciled us to himself by Jesus Christ, and hath given to us the ministry of reconciliation; To wit, that God was in Christ, reconciling the world unto himself, not imputing their trespasses unto them; and hath committed unto us the word of reconciliation."

II Corinthians 5:18-19 KJV

Introduction

"And he said unto him, Oh my Lord, wherewith shall I save Israel? behold, my family is poor in Manasseh, and I am the least in my father's house."

Judges 6:15 KJV

This statement was made thousands of years ago by an Old Testament figure who went by the name of Gideon. When Gideon was approached by the Angel of God, the angel found him hiding in fear from Israel's enemies, the Midianites. However, Gideon was baffled by the angel's greeting.

". . . The Lord is with thee thou mighty man of valour."

Judges 6:12KJV

Just as many who were called by God has done, Gideon immediately proceeded to set the record straight. His response was, there is no way you can be talking to me "my family is poor in Manasseh, and I am the least in my father's house". In other words, I am just an ordinary man. But Gideon was soon to learn, just as I have learned, that God loves to use ordinary people.

"I will praise thee; for I am fearfully and wonderfully made: marvelous are thy works; and that my soul knoweth right well."

Psalms 139:14 KJV

Being an ordinary man, I sometimes find it difficult to try and convey my ideas to others as though I possess some superior knowledge or intellect; especially after taking inventory of my own flaws and shortcomings. With that being said, after years of intense reflection, it has become increasingly clear to me that in spite of our human frailties, all who come this way if only for a moment, have been given by our creator a particular fragment or swatch of this huge puzzle of which only He (God) has the total picture. That's why it's not prudent or wise to argue with Him, when He says this is how a certain thing has to be done, in order for His people to experience a greater degree of fulfillment and purpose in their lives. My purpose here with this treatment is to share revelation, a revealed knowledge. I believe I have received certain incite and knowledge from God because I sought after it. God has placed in me this urge, this quest, this strong desire for divine and infinite knowledge. Therefore, throughout my entire life the question 'why' has been my constant companion.

"If any of you lack wisdom, let him ask of God, that giveth to all men liberally ."

James 1:5 KJV

But how can the finite understand the infinite, and how can the mind of a man comprehend the mind of God? The Apostle Paul, a man inspired by the Spirit of God put it this way.

"This is why I, Paul, am in jail for Christ, having taken up the cause of you outsiders, so-called. I take it that you're familiar with the part I was given in God's plan for including everybody. I got the inside story on this from God himself, as I just wrote you in brief. As you read over what I have written to you, you'll be able to see for yourselves into the mystery of Christ. None of our ancestors understood this. Only in our time has it been made clear by God's Spirit through his holy apostles and prophets of this new order. The mystery is that people who have never heard of God and those who have heard of him all their lives (what I've been calling outsiders and insiders) stand

on the same ground before God. They get the same offer, same help, same promises in Christ Jesus. The Message is accessible and welcoming to everyone, across the board. This is my life work: helping people understand and respond to this Message. It came as a sheer gift to me, a real surprise, God handling all the details. When it came to presenting the Message to people who had no background in God's way, I was the least qualified of any of the available Christians. God saw to it that I was equipped, but you can be sure that it had nothing to do with my natural abilities. And so here I am, preaching and writing about things that are way over my head, the inexhaustible riches and generosity of Christ. My task is to bring out in the open and make plain what God, who created all this in the first place, has been doing in secret and behind the scenes all along. Through followers of Jesus like yourselves gathered in Churches, this extraordinary plan of God is becoming known and talked about even among the angels!"

Ephesians 3:1-10 (The Message)

In these scriptures Paul explains that God had given him a special revelation and stewardship. He makes it clear that this was not something that he himself had earned no more than you or I could earn our place in the Kingdom of God. It is a gift, and the proper response from one receiving such a gift would be to simply say 'thank you' through prayer, praise and worship. I have learned to accept the fact that my journey, as with the journey of all men, was a well orchestrated one that began in the womb of my mother and continues to be fostered and perpetuated to this very day. Now one might ask what of those lives that have been cut short, or have been wrongly or unjustly taken, because the feeling is that they have also suffered loss. But I believe even these events are there to impact the thinking and attitudes of those of us who are left behind. It has been said that one moment with God in heaven is far greater than a lifetime with men on earth.

The idea of this work is that it might be seen as a call to arms and to offer what I have termed the three essentials:

- Enlightenment - an introduction to the truth,
- Encouragement - offers purpose and direction, and
- Empowerment - the strength to continue along this path.

We must be willing to assist those who might be grappling with the demon of confusion, as mankind's biggest frustration is to find the answers to questions like why am I here, and whose idea was this anyway? Many have turned to religion only to end up feeling more confused and betrayed. Christianity has been blamed for causing a degree of uncertainty in so many lives. Small wonder, since it is evident to many observers that the Church herself has seemingly lost her way. Just as there can be no life without blood pumping through one's body, there can be no cohesiveness or singleness of mind for the Christian Church, without a heart or a center.

"Keep thy heart with all diligence; for out of it are the issues of life."
Proverbs 4:23 KJV

And where pray tell is the heart of the Church? Where is the geographical center of its birth?

"And (Jesus) being assembled together with them (the Apostles), commanded them that they should not depart from Jerusalem but wait for the promise of the Father which, saith he, ye have heard of me."
Acts1:4 KJV

And so for the Christian, it would be senseless to debate the fact that if the Church is ever going to reverse its current state of disorientation, we have no recourse but to turn our hearts, minds and prayers towards Jerusalem.

"Pray for the peace of Jerusalem: they shall prosper that love thee."

Psalm 122:6 KJV

The truth is that Christianity is not responsible for the Church's dilemma, but it's the way Christianity has been misrepresented that constitutes the real problem. Especially by those who continue, no matter how subtle, to embrace the practice of anti-Semitism, anti-Judaism or anti-Jerusalem. Let me make it clear that if a substantial part of the Church's involvement and mission, is not geared towards building an alliance and showing our allegiance to Israel, then no matter how innocent our neglect, it is still anti-Semitism, anti-Judaism or anti-Jerusalem.

"He that is not with me is against me: and he that gathered not with me scattereth."

Luke 11:23 KJV

Our biggest battle is with what is called, 'secular humanism'; a system of doctrines and practices that disregards or rejects any form of religious faith and worship.

Some of these people have no problem with Israel's right to be a sovereign nation, but they are in direct opposition to Israel's divine appointment as a beacon of light for the rest of the world. They therefore act as deterrents from the pattern of hope that God has set for us all. May God help us to untangle this web of deceit that has covered the truth, and blinded the minds of many.

Many reject the idea of a superior mind being responsible for the existence of man, but when I look at the magnificent creatures, the tremendous design and the brilliant colors, the birds and fish that only flock and spawn together; when I look at man and his ability to manifest so many emotions and ideas, to be able to build, conquer, plan and create; I refuse to accept the assessment of some person who one day stood up, put his thumbs under his suspenders and announced "after careful consideration, I have determined that there is no God", and that we are all here as the result of some freak happening or cosmic collision. I tell you this, that I would have gladly stood before that man and all who support him, and put my thumbs under my suspenders - if I had some - and declare "there are millions of us who have some say in this matter, and you have to be out of your philosophical mind to think that we would allow all that we are and all that we might become, to be summed up in your human opinion." Whenever I am confronted with the question of Darwin's Big Bang Theory, I always respond with three questions of my own:

- Who or what were the participants in this grand event,
- What force moved them into action, and
- Where did it come from?

I will continue to proclaim to the world that we are not the result of some unforeseen event, but we are the result of divine excellence, and our creator God, is the mastermind of it all.

"Behold I am the Lord,
The God of all Flesh;
Is there anything too hard for me?"

Jeremiah 32:27 KJV

CHAPTER 1

The Journey of a Common Man
"My Own Story"

"And it shall come to pass, that whosoever shall call on the name of the LORD shall be delivered: for in mount Zion and in Jerusalem shall be deliverance, as the LORD hath said, and in the remnant whom the LORD shall call."

Joel 2:32 KJV

This prophetic window and others like it peering into Israel's future, still remains a perplexing enigma to both the people of Israel and to those who have been introduced to Israel's predetermined destiny. They are often left with more questions than answers. Questions like when and how is all this suppose to take place? As always, God remains true to His tradition as He continues to keep men in suspense, until He is ready to reveal His handiwork. That is why we should never take our eyes off of the limitless possibilities of the infinite being God, Him whom we worship.

We know that there are certain people who will be appalled at the idea that as the Church, we would have the audacity to think somehow and in some way, we should get involved in Israel's current state of affairs. However, we are of the Ecclesia - 'a called out remnant' that God has set in place and in motion for this particular point in time. Moreover, our being part of this remnant gives us every right to speak in the way that we do. We are genuinely concerned with Israel's prosperity and well being. It is by God's Holy Spirit that we feel compelled to issue this clarion call to the entire Christian community. "As Israel goes, so goes the rest of the world."

"God that made the world and all things therein, seeing that he is Lord of heaven and earth, dwelleth not in temples made with hands; Neither is worshipped with men's hands, as though he needed any thing, seeing he giveth to all life, and breath, and all things; And hath made of one blood all nations of men for to dwell on all the face of the earth, and hath determined the times before appointed, and the bounds of their habitation."

Acts 17:24-26 KJV

Just as we are familiar with the term 'landlord' as describing a property owner who leases his property to others, so is God Lord of both heaven and earth. Therefore, He should not be minimized in our thoughts towards Him. So often because of the voluminous boundless statute of God, for many it is difficult to imagine the very mind, attention and design of Him trickling down into, and becoming interwoven with the concerns of a common everyday mortal man. Not just at some particular event or juncture in their lives, but from the very moment of their inception. Paul shares with us the definitive linkage that God has with men, and the common linkage that men have with each other – **One Blood.**

Paul is very confident and comfortable with the idea that when it comes to God's created being, man, every step that he makes, every breath that he takes, every inch of ground that he covers, and every person that he meets have all been measured, appointed and determined before time ever was.

When I look back at what appeared to be a mundane existence and life that began without real purpose, I am thoroughly amazed at the fact that God was always around, which is to say no matter how dismal or grim an event or circumstance may appear to be, there has never been a moment or place in time where God was not in attendance.

"And Moses said unto God, Who am I, that I should go unto Pharaoh, and that I should bring forth the children of Israel out of Egypt?"

Exodus 3:11 KJV

Who am I? I honestly can't remember how many times I have found myself asking that very same question, when confronted with challenges that I felt exceeded my ability to perform. Who would have thought that after 40 years of living in exile, this man Moses born of Hebrew slaves, and at the time

3

of this particular event a fugitive in hiding, would be used of God to deliver his people Israel out of Egyptian bondage? At least in Moses' mind, this task that he had been summoned to undertake was both huge and unthinkable.

At Israel's birth Egypt had already had many centuries of stable national life behind her. The Pharaohs were not only the Lords of a dynasty; they were also the patrons of a majestic culture. The pyramids and hieroglyphic inscriptions on walls and tombs showed their intense ambition to preserve, and transmit the Egyptian experience. Massive statues and exquisite mural paintings reflect their artistic imaginations. The political sway of Egypt's strength and power ran from the Nile which is the Sudan, across the Sinai wilderness into Canaan and Syria.Sometimes an Egyptian expedition would reach as far westward as Libya. Moses was born at a time when the Pharaoh, the ruler of Egypt - a most powerful and magnificent dynasty - had given orders that no more male Hebrew children should be allowed to live. The Hebrew slaves had been reproducing so fast that he felt threatened by a Hebrew revolt against his authority. But, in an attempt to save her young child's life, his mother fashioned a basket of papyrus, waterproofed it with asphalt and pitch, and set it afloat on the Nile River. By God's divine providence the child was recovered by a princess who was the daughter of Pharaoh, who would raise him as her own son.

However, unbeknown to the princess in her search to find a nursemaid to rear the child, she chose Moses' own mother who would play a critical role and have tremendous influence inthe life of this young prince of Egypt. Moses' 40 years in Egypt afforded him ample time to learn many things concerning the Egyptian culture, and way of life. Also, I believe at some point during that same time, he struggled with his inner most feelings concerning the accepted practices of how the Jews then called Hebrews, were to be treated. In a fit of anger Moses took the life of an Egyptian soldier for beating a Hebrew slave and this led to his banishment from the Land.

The Bible's depiction of Moses' first encounter with God makes it apparent that his approach to "this great sight", (a burning bush), was that of a curious observer. Little did he know that he was being led down a path that God had set in place for him long before he was ever born.

"Remember the former things of old: for I am God, and there is none else; I am God, and there is none like me, Declaring the end from the beginning, and from ancient times the things that are not yet done, saying, My counsel shall stand, and I will do all my pleasure."

Isaiah 46:9-10 KJV

I can certainly connect with Moses' dilemma during that time. His feelings of compassion that were born out of a place that was not easily identifiable, and his feelings of frustration which derived from knowing what should be done, but not knowing exactly how to do it.

"And now we are rising from the ashes and we are putting forth our hands look inside us for our story, see through our eyes and understand". (A gift from an Indian friend)

Being the 17th of 18 children, it is needless to say that I too have witnessed a lot of frustrations growing up on the streets of Washington, DC. I was only six weeks old when my parents migrated to the city from Raleigh, North Carolina. I guess you could say that I was a Washingtonian to the bone. There was a time when I would say that with a lot of pride, but these days I'm not so sure. So much has changed to the detriment of the generations that are coming up behind us. One need not give a long lengthy analogy of the problems because they are so obvious that almost any inner city child can recite them. What's even more disturbing to me as I look back on certain things, is the distinct possibility that many of these young children, may be the victims of an empty fruitless legacy passed on to them by the prior generation - my generation. Although we did not intend to leave them without substance, certainly the old adage *"I didn't know the gun was loaded"* can be applied here.

The reason why I say this is because as a people, at least up to this point we are still divided in America. While on the other hand, the unity of the Hebrew nation has been sustained throughout the ages by a vision of descent from a single ancestor. The narrative in Genesis of Abraham, Isaac and Jacob is presented in the language of national pride. It evokes the memory of an age in which God walked intimately with men and intervened in the daily commerce of their lives. A spiritually inspired Moses chronicles the biblical account, that tells us Abraham received divine instructions to leave his land and kinsmen for a new country, one in which he would found a historic lineage of his own. Obedient to the divine voice, Abraham moved into Western Palestine – the land of the Canaanites, the territory from Dan to Beersheba is promised to him as an inheritance. I don't know what kinds of things Moses' mother whispered in his ear as he was growing up in Egypt. I can still remember so vividly the things my mother whispered in my ear as she tried to shield us from the evil that she knew existed beyond the boundaries of our neighborhood Projects. (That's what our living areas where called – The Projects). Sounded like some kind of testing or breeding ground for manual laborers. At least that's what it seemed like to those of us who were of the then younger generation. So we had made up our minds that when we grew up into adulthood, we would definitely do some things differently. We decided that we would be more prepared and prepare our children as well, not to be drawn into the trap which we called an "attitude of servitude". As much as our parents tried to protect us, there was an alluring bitter sweet passion in the air, a longing to get on the other side of the street where the grass always seemed greener. Oftentimes, we couldn't get to it but it sure managed to get to us through our music. The music made us want things and we were left with the question of how to get them. Mistakes, mistakes, mistakes or should I say tricked again.

• The first trick was for us to think that we knew more than our parents, which meant that any personal or direct link to the historical account of our plight was broken, and we found ourselves mobilizing in an endless cycle of starting over again.

• The second trick was that we didn't understand the nature of the forces that were working against us.

So even though in my father's house, the predominant un-compromising message was that of love and caring, we hadn't yet learned to appreciate the wisdom that our parents had acquired over the years. Neither did we comprehend the unique challenges they faced trying to raise an entire football team complete with cheerleaders. Eighteen children, that's a lot of folk!

It goes without saying that my father worked hard to keep a roof over our heads, but I believe that my mother worked doubly hard trying to hold down the roost until he got home in the evening. My mother was a strong beautiful woman of Cherokee Indian descent. In fact, she was born on an Indian reservation in Spring Hope, North Carolina. So there were many nights when my dad got home he would find his lovely soft spoken wife on the warpath. Needless to say, those were the times when his poor innocent children were so grateful to see his face, and to feel his long callous fingers on theirs.

We were a very close knit family and I would not trade one moment of those times we shared together. However, there still remained the call of the wild, because at the same time my father was instructing me on certain principles for living, there was another message being taught. The message was simple, that despite the passage of five civil rights bills, despite the erosion of illegal support for segregated institutions, despite greater acceptance of blacks into our major institutions, both private and public, it was still no easy thing to be a black person in America. So much time has passed and so little has changed. Like so many others, I sought all kinds of ways, solutions and alternatives to compensate for some of the pain I felt. Pain from the deprivation and humiliation that I and my father and his father before him had suffered, we wanted retribution. In our minds, that retribution could only come in one form, rebellion.

But here again, not understanding the particularities of the battle that was more spiritual than natural, we chose to rebel by re-defining ourselves. Many changed their names and allowed their hair to grow long and wore African attire purchased primarily from street vendors and Korean merchants. We used African slogans and batted around the African words we had learned mainly from each other. Now with the identity change we needed a change of attitude; something that would drown out the warnings of our elders and those who would lead us down the path of submission. In walked the mind altering drugs. We had fallen into a perilous pit face down and the more we dug in the deeper we sank, carrying with us everyone who believed that we had the plan. I cannot remember how many pro black organizations I belonged to, but, through it all somehow, this thing that my father had instilled in me kept haunting me and getting in my way. It heightened my compassion and concern for the needs of others. I soon realized that somehow through the blood, all of us would be tied together forever. This is why I needed to understand how a man like him could love unconditionally in the way that he did. How could he give food and money away to other families when often times we had so little ourselves; and why did he walk up and put himself in harms way, getting in the middle of disputes and fights, risking life and limb while acting as a mediator, many times while the participants were still brandishing weapons.

When I accompanied him on trips to the market places he would shake hands and hug and kiss strangers and babies, as if he were running for public office. This man clearly had a sincere concern for his fellow man and an uncanny love for the Jewish people and the Nation of Israel. It was also apparent that a lot of things that would insult or intimidate most people and make them feel disconnected or disenfranchised did not bother him. He was able to roll through those things and keep his head up as this tall proud individual in an environment that normally had been hostile, by insisting that he accept his assignment as a substandard human being. He became a king, so much so that many of the Jewish shop keepers would offer him gifts, and bare their souls to him and seek his counsel. They recognized that this was a man among men. It was not until later years that I realized that his ability to do those things came as the direct result of him embracing a bigger picture, one in which he was also included. He had risen above the natural and ascended to a higher plain, and there in fellowship with God he found purpose; a purpose which was rooted and grounded in both an idea and solution, neither of which would ever fade away.

"For to be carnally minded is death; but to be spiritually minded is life and peace."
Romans 8:6

This was vital to his success as a God man. By divorcing myself from my father's teachings, I had become material minded, because in our neck of the woods a man was measured by the things he possessed. In truth, the further I got away from my father's teachings, the further I got away from God's divine purpose for my life. As time has shown, God continues to place in our midst those who would yield to the call upon their lives of

9

mentoring others. My father was certainly one of these people. If the truth be told there are still so many others both Jew and Gentile, who have never recognized the power and plan of God waiting to be birthed in their lives.

"For whom he did foreknow, he also did predestinate to be conformed to the image of his Son, that he might be the firstborn among many brethren. Moreover whom he did predestinate, them he also called: and whom he called, them he also justified: and whom he justified, them he also glorified. What shall we then say to these things? If God be for us, who can be against us?"
Romans 8:29-31 KJV

I know that without a doubt I am a man under grace. One who in the eyes of men might be so undeserving, but because grace is a different kind of movement, maneuver, action or idea, I remained in the game. Grace can only be understood and interpreted through the heart. In other words, if you have never known love then you will never understand grace. I have always defined love as when one is willing to make tremendous sacrifices for others or another without looking for anything in return. I must admit that although I understand love, I cannot perform it in the same way God does. Sometimes as a man I get trapped by my own human emotions while harboring a concern that in giving my all, I don't give too much. There is also the temptation to judge an individual based on the way they are currently conducting business. Now God does bring about change, but he always begins by taking us as and where we are.

"For by one Spirit are we all baptized into one body, whether we be Jews or Gentiles, whether we be bond or free; and have been all made to drink into one Spirit."
1 Corinthians 12:13 KJV

It's a fact, that people from all spheres of life are feeling what I am saying now. We are all here because God deposited us here, and we need to follow Him and His plan for this hour. The Apostle makes it clear that this end time spiritual surge – baptism – will fall upon believers as well as those who are currently unbelievers, to produce what Paul calls the one body.

"Take my yoke upon you, and learn of me; for I am meek and lowly in heart: and ye shall find rest unto your souls."
Matthew 11:29 KJV

Through the scriptures we are requested to hold our judgment against God and His Christ, until we have first given them the benefit of learning who they really are. These words were written by the Old Testament Jewish prophet Jeremiah.

"And ye shall seek me, and find me, when ye shall search for me with all your heart."
Jeremiah 29:13 KJV

We are encouraged to take this unchartered journey which will ultimately bring us face to face with God. The only criteria is that we have a sincere desire to know Him, and what He had in mind for our lives when He commissioned us to be here. I want my readers to see this as a journey through the eyes of an ordinary man, one who was drawn to God by His truths and His truths alone. There were no plans for financial gain or prominent recognition, just a desire to get closer to an idea that I knew some men might never grasp.

CHAPTER 2

The Dispersion of a Bloodline

*"O magnify the LORD with me, and let us exalt his name to-
gether. I sought the LORD, and he heard me, and delivered me
from all my fears. They looked unto him, and were lightened:
and their faces were not ashamed."*

Psalm 34:3-5 KJV

This psalm was written by King David concerning an incident where he was captured by the Philistine King Achish,
while being pursued by those of the house of King Saul. David's
plan of escape was definitely a unique one. Immediately after
being captured David "feigned himself mad" which turned out
to be a good idea. Once it was determined by the King that David was not a threat nor was he in possession of the mental fac-
ulties to cause any future problems, David was released. Now
the question that will go unanswered is whose idea was it to
fake madness, David's or God's? David who feared for his life
wrote, "I sought the Lord, and he heard me, and delivered me
from all my fears". For most people it's difficult to fathom God
operating outside of the box, even though He is the Creator not
only of the box, but all of its perimeters.

*"O the depth of the riches both of the wisdom and knowledge of
God! How unsearchable are his judgments, and his ways past
finding out!"*

Romans 11:33

This can be seen by paralleling the plights of two nations
of people, the black African Nation and the Jewish Nation of
Israel. History records that the almost mythical endurance and
pronounced destinies of these two nations were always inter-
twined.

*"Are ye not as children of the Ethiopians unto me, O children of
Israel? saith the Lord."*

Amos 9:7

We believe that along with the many powerful gifted members of other ethnic groups, who have been on the front lines for years and will no doubt play major roles in this progressive movement, the people of African descent will also have a tremendous impact on Israel's victorious future.

"For I would not, brethren, that ye should be ignorant of this mystery, lest ye should be wise in your own conceits; that blindness in part is happened to Israel, until the fullness of the Gentiles be come in. And so all Israel shall be saved..."
                                                              Romans 11:25-26 KJV

One sure fire way to ignite controversy in the African American community would be to suggest, even remotely, that the ill treatment of blacks in America and the involuntary disbursement of the African bloodline globally, would be somehow directly connected with God's end time plan for Israel, Africa and ultimately the entire world. As the old saying goes, "you can't fairly judge a man until you have walked a mile in his shoes." If there is one group that can understand the feelings that are being harbored by Jews around the world, it is the African Nation. The feelings of betrayal and resentment over being a targeted group; the fear of the past repeating itself in certain areas; the need to try and determine who their true allies are; and how dangerous it is to continue to ignore obvious signs that your enemies are refueling their hatred and aggressions against you.

This unprecedented, unheralded awakening toward reconciliation is going to require a sincere crying out to God on the part of the true Church concerning the peace of Jerusalem. *"They shall prosper that love thee."*

This must come in the form of service through prayer, praise and worship. One fact that cannot be ignored is the ability of blacks to bear their souls before God. The single most attribute that allowed blacks to maintain their sanity, in the midst of all

15

the madness that engulfed them, was this imbedded gift that enabled them to lift their spirits above the shackles of their pain. They learned very quickly and out of necessity that an inspirational song brings the soul to the surface, where it can be readily ministered to. Prayers, praise, worship, and rhythm to those who are of the African bloodline is as fluent and easy as breathing.

One of the many things that God shows His mastery at is His incredible ability to recover plights and situations long after they have passed the *'point of no return'*. While everyone else has thrown up their hands and abandoned all hopes that this particular predicament could ever see the light of day, God shows up. And as if to reverse time, He brings about the kinds of results that would cause those who witness it to sit in awe and wonder what just happened. These kinds of amazing feats that are so faith inspiring, causes those of us who have experienced life changing events to cry from the depths of our souls, all praises to the one true and living God. Isaiah the Prophet has enlightened us to the fact that God is indeed the architect and designer of both good and evil. So, we need not ask what gives God the right, power and authority to do these kinds of things.

Now I know to some that it might seem to be a dismal or bleak thing to consider, but the bible tells us that God chastens those that He loves, and sometimes that chastisement can appear to be a real evil thing. He has a way of making us uncomfortable in order to move us towards His divine design.

"Blessed are ye, when men shall revile you, and persecute you, and shall say all manner of evil against you falsely, for my sake. Rejoice, and be exceeding glad: for great is your reward in heaven: for so persecuted they the prophets which were before you."

Matthew 5:11-12 KJV

These words were spoken by Jesus to a group of Jews who were under heavy persecution inflicted upon them by Roman dictatorship. Needless to say, that his words probably seemed a little insensitive when it came to addressing their current situation.

Once again, you can sense God operating within His own timeframe, as he clearly contemplates or nurtures a broader agenda. An agenda that extends far beyond our individual priorities or what works best for us at the moment. And, so it is with the African American community in this country. I am convinced that unlike any time in recent history, blacks through the Church will have a profound effect on Israel's divine prospects and well being.

"But ye are a chosen generation, a royal priesthood, an holy nation, a peculiar people; that ye should shew forth the praises of him who hath called you out of darkness into his marvellous light: Which in time past were not a people, but are now the people of God: which had not obtained mercy, but now have obtained mercy."

1Peter 2:9-10 KJV

The universal Church with its entire ethnic flavor will be highlighted, siding with Israel against her enemies both spiritual and natural. As we move forward we will be able to identify the similarities between Jews and blacks and the irrefutable kinship they share. From the Black perspective, it is true that the gains of the Civil Rights movement in the sixties were important for that time when it was vigorously being pursued. However, these efforts in and of themselves would not be enough.

"Though thy beginning was small, yet thy latter end should greatly increase."

Job 8:7 KJV

17

We are grateful that some did not fall through the cracks and were able to move on and do fairly well for themselves. Many became giants in the areas of medicine, business, science, journalism, politics, and the arts. But because we have seen how blood ties, it is safe to surmise that the grand or broader mission of this bloodline had not yet reached fruition. Although some had managed to remove themselves far from the scenes of Black despair, all Blacks like Jews are still identified with one racial group. The difference being, however, that unlike Jews, Blacks as a group are still powerless, impoverished, and unable to compete without enduring some kind of social or financial handicap or handout in America. As a result of the Civil Rights era, we were able to sit at a lunch counter and vote. But economically, Civil Rights gains took much more from us than it gave.

The Vietnamese, Koreans, Indians, Iranians, and Mexicans were putting up profitable businesses in our neighborhoods, and we were still hopelessly vulnerable to every danger, from police brutality to violence and poverty. It still boggles my imagination to think that all of these modern atrocities stem from what historians, politicians, and social scientists have referred to as "*a peculiar institution*-**The American Slave Trade.**" Now the practice of human enslavement is a phenomenon of mankind that extends back to prehistoric times. But the enslavement of Black people in America clearly dispersed a critical bloodline, and has been so totally unique in its role, scope and consequence, that these observers of human behavior considered it very peculiar. It defied all excepted religious precepts and secular standards of normative behavior. In other words, it was and to some still is mystifying.

The sheer number of people enslaved was unprecedented; an estimated 50 million to 60 million blacks were captured in Africa for enslavement. More than 35 million died en-route to various ports, with approximately 15 million actually reaching the slave markets.

Black slavery was purely and simply racial and economic exploitation that caused an economic revolution and entrenched disparities between Blacks and Whites; leaving Blacks feeling for centuries that all that remained for them were empty promises. We had further handicapped ourselves by some of our beliefs and behaviors. Our intense pursuit of integration is one example. In so doing, we had destroyed our communities, diluted our numerical strength and became dependent upon others. We had clearly reached a *'point of no return'*. We couldn't grasp the concept that because the roof was leaking or that there was paper or rags in the windows where glass should have been, didn't mean that the people inside were beyond redemption or recovery.

We had little Churches on almost every corner, but as a people of one bloodline, we never looked toward heaven for answers. Our progress was further impeded by our inability to practice group economics in a capitalistic democracy. We have always been a key capitalistic element in the national empowerment plans of others, as a source of cheap labor and in the spending of our dollars. Yet we have never had a national empowerment plan of our own. All of this only lends support to my earlier assertion that the fact that there are still too many Black children who have been left trying to cope with a broken down legacy, wields as a dagger in the heart of black America, or should I say in the heart of America as a whole.

Now let me make it clear, that in no way am I suggesting that the contributions of those who led in the Civil Rights movement are less than noble. Certainly, because of the tremendous sacrifices they made and extraordinary courage they exhibited, their names and exploits will always be attached to the legacy and highlights of the American experience. But what I am saying is from that experience, there is much more to be garnered.

First of all, we must be willing to admit that at some point we dropped the ball. As a group, we did not pass the baton on to another prepared younger group. An effort, that started fully trusting in God, became the work of men. After the death of Dr. King, personal recognition, ambitions and agendas, soon took the place of humble submission. We walked away from our most substantial resource - God. It is my contention that as a chosen generation, and as a part of His elect remnant, we must return to Him and seek His endowment. There are just too many negative forces at work for us to try and go it alone. More importantly, we must all understand that our greater concerns are no longer just a matter of differences between races. Our immediate apprehensions must be broader and inclusive in scope. When the people who were responsible for the Trade Center bombings set out to bring those two buildings down, not once did they consider who might have been inside. There were Whites, Blacks, Jews, Asians, Mexicans and even Muslims,but to our enemies, it was all about the spilling of American blood. We all know that there is a lot of healing that must take place concerning race in this country. This healing must begin with me and it has to begin with you. As a nation called of God we have a lot of rethinking and repositioning to do.

At the height of the American Slave Trade, even the Churches turned their backs on the truth. The Catholic Churches support of Black slavery was second only to the Muslim Arabs. The Catholic Order not only justified Black slavery, but was a major owner of slaves. In 1488, Pope Innocent VIII, accepted a gift of one hundred Moorish slaves from Ferdinand of Spain and then distributed the slaves to various Cardinals and Nobles. The Protestant religion in America, have always reflected the value and practices of the dominant white society. Beginning in 1619 the Protestant denominations accepted and supported secular decisions to enslave and exploit Blacks as a separate labor class for developing a white nation.

They even taught that in the present world, Blacks were inferior beings. Faithful slaves were to except their lot in life, be obedient to their white masters, and their souls would find equality with whites in the next world.

During biblical times the Hebrews owned and were slaves, which go to show, that just as some Black tribes in Africa, they have known both sides of the coin. The degree of Jewish involvement in modern black slave trading and exploitation of Blacks is heatedly debated. At one point, the Washington Post cited extensive research by Jewish historians who claimed that Jews were involved in nearly every aspect of Black slavery, including slave traders, financiers of slavery and confederate war supporters. The Post article also claimed that Jews owned slave vessels, textile mills and tobacco plantations. Again, those claims have been disputed by many Jewish organizations and groups.

But there is one fact that can not be disputed, the fact that it has often been a conclusion of popular history that Blacks and Jews have always shared a strong alliance. At various times abolitionist, liberals, and individual Jews have provided visible support to black causes and some times at great personal risk and expense. They have lobbied state and federal legislative branches of government, contributed financial resources, provided surrogate leadership and given their lives to assist Blacks in their efforts to become free.

Still, sometime ago I set out to state the case of a violated people before God. I even pinned this poem and circulated it whenever and wherever I could.

21

When tribalism deemed that together we stood,
God gave us the land and all things were good.
With no need to ravish my brother, for my household too had plenty,
Acts of greed and violence were few indeed if any.
Equal beauty we shared in appearance
discarding a need for lust,
and this oneness we had provided
a foundation for pure love and trust.
When to our shores came strange men of wonder
With sticks of fire that spoke like thunder,
what manner of man had skin like the light
hair like a lion and caused much more fright?
His eyes bore the colors of evil,
like the serpents we all knew too well,
and his message of death and destruction
came straight from the ruins of Hell.
But as screams of pain split the silence of night,
and we watched our Villages burn;
God's message too was unfolding
one that he was destined to learn.
That dependence on us would befall him
As we grew in numbers and mind,
and our oneness would always prevail
out of pure love for self and kind.
And though Our History here in this country
is filled mostly with blood, sweat and pains
our Queens proved to be twice his equal,
and bore Kings in spite of their chains.
They brought his books to the small ones,
and shoved giants through his front doors
and while holding this all together
still found time for his weak woman's chores.
And from our National Hymn,
Lift Every Voice,
until our people will no longer starve,
The truth rings clear, we have no choice
But to L - O - V - E; Let Our Virtues Evolve
                    Author, R L Woods

In my feeble attempt to challenge the loathsome injustices and heinous crimes that had been leveled against us, and had disrupted our bloodline, God dazzled me with both His wisdom and compassion.

First He allowed me to go on a search to try and understand how it could be that men, who have always been linked together by the same blood, could view themselves, others and the world around them so differently. What I discovered was a matter of science, and this science is just another means of defining and monitoring God's movements. What I also learned was that even though blood is the single link that ties all of mankind together, there is something called the genetic code that qualifies the characteristics of a particular ethnic group. The term "genetic" is the scientific designation for the genesis -- beginning or origin of something. The science of genetics is the branch of biology that deals with heredity and variation in similar or related animals or plants. It includes the genetic features of an individual group or kind. The genetic code is the order in which four chemical constituents are arranged in huge molecules of DNA, an essential component of all cells. All of this has a direct bearing on how an individual, group, or kind, will interact with its environment and the rest of the people who are in it.

Needless to say, this is an astounding revelation and testament to how deep, thorough and complex our God really is.

"Now there are diversities of gifts, but the same Spirit. And there are differences of administrations, but the same Lord. And there are diversities of operations, but it is the same God which worketh all in all."
I Corinthians 12:4-6 KJV

It's from these diverse groups that God will assemble His remnant pool, with each ethnic group making its contribution to the pool. These believers will stand as a monument to the sovereign and supreme rulership of God; survivors who are able to relinquish their will for His.

"Even so then at this present time also there is a remnant according to the election of grace."

Romans 11:5 KJV

The second thing God did, rather than answer my appeal for justice, was to simply set before me all the things that I had done in my prior life. One by one, they marched through my mind like a cloud of witnesses that could bring a judge, even a righteous judge, to only one verdict, *"Guilty as charged."* Then I heard God say "be not overwhelmed by those things my son, for I have forgiven all", so that you might be an example and do likewise. If you will forgive, I will show you my plan concerning Israel and the true Church. This will be a glimmering testimony to the nations of the world, when the two finally become one.

"For if ye forgive men their trespasses, your heavenly Father will also forgive you: But if ye forgive not men their trespasses, neither will your Father forgive your trespasses."

Matthew 6:14-15 KJV

As far as I am concerned on the subject of forgiveness, for me that book has been closed.
I FORGIVE ALL.

CHAPTER 3

The God of Increase

"The heavens declare the glory of God; and the firmament sheweth his handywork."

Psalm 19:1 KJV

And so begins our amazing journey into the awesome plan and mind of God just as He promised. From here in order to launch this astonishing sojourn, our first step must be towards His breathtaking design. A design which in and of itself is beyond human comprehension. At the onset, there is nothing in our region but God. Then He speaks and it's on and it's beautiful and good.

"In the beginning God created the heaven and the earth."

Genesis 1:1 KJV

But that's just the beginning... in the next movement of scripture, we're introduced to the first created being on earth, man.

"And God said, Let us make man in our image, after our likeness: and let them have dominion over the fish of the sea, and over the fowl of the air, and over the cattle, and over all the earth, and over every creeping thing that creepeth upon the earth. So God created man in his own image, in the image of God created he him; male and female created he them."

Genesis 1:26-27 KJV

Science tells us that for every action there is a reaction. God's spoken words, "Let there be light", was the action and the formation of all creation was the reaction to His command. For every cause there is an effect, God was the cause and man was the effect.

One would think that this unmatched display of design and creativity would be enough, but it wasn't over yet. To all of this beauty, bountifulness and splendor, God adds a wrinkle. Another player, this dark force which would act as a disputant,

attacker, assailant, a gamester, adversary, and antagonist called
Lucifer. First he shows up in the garden as a serpent.

*"Now the serpent was more subtil than any beast of the field
which the Lord God had made. And he said unto the woman,
Yea, hath God said, Ye shall not eat of every tree of the garden?"*

Genesis 3:1 KJV

But later he is formally introduced to us by the Jewish Prophets Isaiah and Ezekiel.

*"How art thou fallen from heaven, O Lucifer, son of the morn-
ing! how art thou cut down to the ground, which didst weaken
the nations!"*

Isaiah 14:12 KJV

*"Thou hast been in Eden the garden of God; every precious stone
was thy covering, the sardius, topaz, and the diamond, the
beryl, the onyx, and the jasper, the sapphire, the emerald, and
the carbuncle, and gold: the workmanship of thy tabrets and of
thy pipes was prepared in thee in the day that thou wast created. Thou art the anointed cherub that covereth; and I have set
thee so: thou wast upon the holy mountain of God; thou hast
walked up and down in the midst of the stones of fire. Thou
wast perfect in thy ways from the day that thou wast created,
till iniquity was found in thee."*

Ezekiel 28:13-15 KJV

In an attempt to try to get a handle on this incredible procre-
ation, let us now fast forward into the future.

*"After this I beheld, and, lo, a great multitude, which no man
could number, of all nations, and kindreds, and people, and
tongues, stood before the throne, and before the Lamb, clothed
with white robes, and palms in their hands; And cried with a*

loud voice, saying, Salvation to our God which sitteth upon the throne, and unto the Lamb."

Revelation 7:9-10 KJV

Here in Revelation, we get a glimpse into eternity where an untold number of people are voluntarily praising God in response to some unforgettable feat that He had performed in their lives. So we have the beginning and we have the ending. The only thing left is the strategy in the middle complete with its checks and balances, which later would be referred to as light against darkness right against wrong, and good against evil. But through it all, God would leave no doubt as to who the architect of this entire universal system was.

"I form the light, and create darkness: I make peace, and create evil: I the LORD do all these things. Drop down, ye heavens, from above, and let the skies pour down righteousness: let the earth open, and let them bring forth salvation, and let righteousness spring up together; I the LORD have created it"

Isaiah 45:7-8 KJV

This proclamation from Jehovah Elohim (The Creator), makes it unanimously clear, "I the Lord do all these things." No matter how it may appear that God's plan for His chosen people Israel has been derailed, in reality nothing could be further from the truth. Even though the Church may not currently be walking in that which was given her, Gods gifts are without repentance. No man can claim to know all there is to know about God. It would be a fundamental impossibility. However, He has given us enough to assemble a vivid snapshot of what His intensions are and the vastness of His being. One thing is certain, that nothing can sidetrack any purpose or plan that God has set in motion before the foundation of this world. It doesn't matter how many obstacles it might face or how many challenges have to be met, whenever God issues a decree it will ultimately come to pass. The stage has long been set to bring true believers into a oneness first with themselves, their brethren (Jew/Gentile), and eventually with their creator God. At the root of all of this, God has set in place both an idea and a solution. The idea is **love**, the solution is **Blood**.

"For all the law is fulfilled in one word, even in this; Thou shalt love thy neighbour as thyself."
                                            Galatians 5:14 KJV

This is the entire idea.

"For the life of the flesh is in the blood: and I have given it to you upon the altar to make an atonement for your souls: for it is the blood that maketh an atonement for the soul."
                                            Leviticus 17:11 KJV

This is the entire solution.

   Consider these words written by the Apostle Paul concerning the expansion of the Jerusalem Church to include the Gentiles.

"For when the Gentiles, which have not the law, do by nature the things contained in the law, these, having not the law, are a law unto themselves."
                                            Romans 2:14 KJV

   This scripture confirms that God works from the inside out, and it is His Spirit that implements the process by which, a person can be transformed from rags to riches or rubble to righteousness. This Spirit allows them to face down those things that have held them in bondage; things such as fear, hatred, prejudice, anti-Semitism, indifference, or unforgiveness. *Bless God that through the blood we don't have to remain in those places any longer.* We have been given our release from the God of Increase. To increase is to grow in size, degree or amount, to multiply by producing offspring. These words were spoken to the Hebrew patriarch Abraham in the book of Genesis.

"That in blessing I will bless thee, and in multiplying I will multiply thy seed as the stars of the heaven, and as the sand which is upon the sea shore; and thy seed shall possess the gate of his enemies."

Genesis 22:17 KJV

Abraham we are told was willing to offer up to God as a blood sacrifice, his beloved son Isaac. God's response to this unselfish act was to promise, "that in blessing I will bless thee, and in multiplying I will multiply thy seed. "

The fact that God has much to offer and the right and authority to do so, is exemplified in the Old Testament Book of Psalms.

"But our God is in the heavens: he hath done whatsoever he hath pleased."

Psalm 115:3 KJV

The implication here is that all one has to do is lift up their head on a star filled night and gaze into what is obviously infinity. And if there was some doubt or question about God's vastness or His greatness, that particular issue should be resolved. As we are admonished by another Old Testament Psalms which says,

"The fool hath said in his heart, There is no God..."

Psalm 14:1 KJV

If there is a God, then surely He has a plan and a time for that plan to be executed. No matter how radical it may appear to be to some, it is more than obvious that the time is now and the plan has been set before us. We are not being entertained by the antics of a few uninformed, over zealous modern day Christians. This huge drama has been in the makings for a long, long time; from the smallest minuet detail to the grandest of all scales.

"All flesh is not the same flesh: but there is one kind of flesh of men, another flesh of beasts, another of fishes, and another of birds. There are also celestial bodies and bodies terrestrial: but the glory of the celestial is one, and the glory of the terrestrial is another. There is one glory of the sun, and another glory of the moon, and another glory of the stars: for one star differeth from another star in glory."
I Corinthians 15:39-41 KJV

None can deny that God's thinking is much larger than the human mind can truly comprehend. The mind starts to boggle even at the distances of our neighboring stars. Some stars are even light years away. A light year is the distance light travels in one year, 5.87 trillion miles. Scientists and astrologists are still trying to chart what they call the local neighborhood, which they say extends to a radius of 5,000 light years from our solar system. And this is still only a fraction of the entire milky-way which is more than ten times larger.

No one knows how long this has been going on, but estimates for some older star clusters range from fifty million to ten billion years and beyond. The larger of these being called the Andromeda Galaxy, and all of this is just a tiny fraction of what our God is working on. (Hallelujah) Now in the midst of this, in our immediate neighborhood, an area called an inner solar system, about 93 million miles from its one sun, orbits the third planet Earth. Like Mercury, Venus and Mars, Earth is a terrestrial world, a solid sphere made mostly of silicates and metals. It is the largest known example of this class of planet. It is unlike any other in its composition, its climate and its support of life as we know and understand it. Earth's blessed atmosphere traps just the right amount of solar energy to raise the ground temperature comfortably above the freezing point of water. Its distance from the sun allows for conditions that are conducive to the presence of liquid surface water. These two factors ensure that well over two-thirds of our planet's surface is covered with water. This is the key to earth's ability to be an incubator of life.

If it were slightly cooler or hotter, the water would have frozen solid or else evaporated a long time ago, and without water to refresh us where would mankind be? Now for the best part, our planet earth is enshrouded or covered if you will, in a blanket of ionized gas called plasma sphere or plasma, which interestingly enough is the same name given to the liquid portion of blood.

Curiously, it seems that the idea of a blood covering has always been ushered to the forefront of man's thinking as part of God's universal plan.

That's why some of us get so excited when we read Scriptures like those found in the Book of Psalms.

"Many, O LORD my God, are thy wonderful works which thou hast done, and thy thoughts which are to us-ward: they cannot be reckoned up in order unto thee: if I would declare and speak of them, they are more than can be numbered."

Psalm 40:5 KJV

"He telleth the number of the stars; he calleth them all by their names. Great is our Lord, and of great power: his understanding is infinite."

Psalm 147:4-5 KJV

We stand in total agreement with the writer of these Psalms, who is captivated and swept away by the idea that this all powerful, all knowing God; perfect and present God is my God. And that this God for whom there are no formulas or devices to measure His fullness, has thoughts about us. We are always on His infinitely divine mind. Just think, all of those stars, and He is not only able to call them out, that is to create them, but He is also able to name them one by one.

This speaks not only to his ability, but to His willingness as well to interact with that which He has created. This is a tremendous commodity, knowing that as we forge ahead we are never without the protection, strength and guidance of El-Shaddai (God Almighty) and His love toward us.

"When thou goest, it shall lead thee; when thou sleepest, it shall keep thee; and when thou awakest, it shall talk with thee."
Proverbs 6:22 KJV

Chapter 4

A Call to Worship

"But our God is in the heavens: he hath done whatsoever he hath pleased. Their idols are silver and gold, the work of men's hands. They have mouths, but they speak not: eyes have they, but they see not: They have ears, but they hear not: noses have they, but they smell not: They have hands, but they handle not: feet have they, but they walk not: neither speak they through their throat. They that make them are like unto them; so is every one that trusteth in them."

Psalms 115:3-8

Let's talk about gods. We know all too well that there are other gods. Gods made with men's hands that only lead them away from their true purpose. Throughout the Old Testament we have been cautioned against them and those who promote them and their dead end results, *"and they that make them are just like them."* Wherever they started out that's where they end up. That's why some people don't move, don't change; they generally keep the same things they have always had; attitudes, habits, downfalls and prejudices. The things that they treasure or embrace don't grow spiritually. The gods that they worship are dead. Our God is a God of revelation, always presenting us with new ideas and approaches. Of course they are not new to Him because they have always been around. But when we receive them they are usually awesome by design and range. One question we are always asked, how can a loving God allow so many people to suffer the way that He does? That question can only be answered by those of us who understand God's plan of escape for those whom He has chosen. The path of intimacy with God has always been through pain, suffering and adversity. When we cry out to God, it is because we know that He is there and that He will answer.

This same path has the reverse effect on those who have not been introduced to the living God. Their hopes have been dashed or they are left feeling unguarded or unprotected. These feelings are internalized, causing their senses to be dulled and their thinking to become mechanical. The only information they are able to process is that which comes through natural senses such as the eyes, ears and touch. In other words, if I can't see or feel it, then its not. This limits them in their ability to perceive or see beyond those things that challenge who they are.

"For by him were all things created, that are in heaven, and that are in earth, visible and invisible, whether they be thrones, or dominions, or principalities, or powers: all things were created by him, and for him: And he is before all things, and by him all things consist."

Colossians 1:16-17

This tells us once again that God is in fact the Spiritual engineer of all things. He *is* also a shaker and a mover. He is always shaking people and moving them around. And it's during those times, more than ever, that we should try and strive not to lose our faith. Though circumstances are threatening to bury us, I have learned that sometimes God will allow us to appear to be sinking, just to prove that with Him we can rise again.

"And he said, Lord God, whereby shall I know that I shall inherit it?"

Genesis 15:8

So often, as is the case with God, his plan for Abraham went far beyond what the eyes or the mind of a man could foresee. Oftentimes God will call us to things that we just can't see. As the story goes, Abraham had a concern because God had made blood and blood ties a vital fact of life. Abraham was greatly disturbed over the fact that God had promised him great things, not only for himself, but for his seed, and their seed after them.

The problem, at least in Abraham's mind, was that there were no heirs to receive and carry on after he was gone. He knew that he and his wife were much too old to conceive children of their own. God begins to dialogue with him and establish his faith through experience. Most often we focus all of our attention on the rough moments of the most trying events in our lives. It's a natural response to trouble, fear, doubt or concern. As I have already stated, most of us can look back at those times when we were convinced that there was no solution to our problem. This was in fact the big one, but lo and behold the blood prevailed and we got out. Oftentimes we were not expecting it and in many cases didn't even request it. But because the love of God and His purpose for our lives still remained, we survived. This is what God reminded Abraham of, that He had called him out from an unbelieving people, who were worshipping idol gods. Abraham's human skepticism had kicked in. Though God does not want us to rely on human feelings when it comes to His promises, He will indulge us. God's response to Abraham's question, *"how shall I know that I shall inherit it?"*, was to request a sacrifice.

"And he said unto him, Take me an heifer of three years old, and a she goat of three years old, and a ram of three years old, and a turtledove, and a young pigeon."

Genesis 15:9

In other words, turn all of your attention towards me and what I have instructed you to do, and I will richly bless you. If you are earnestly coming before God, you should not do so without bringing with you something that has substance and value. Part of our obligation to serve is to step out by faith into unchartered waters. Let me state emphatically that there is an enormous difference between celebrating God and serving Him. To celebrate God is to elevate, amplify and magnify Him. To serve Him is to be willing to reach out and touch someone else's pain.

There are just too many of us who want to be, without becoming. God is looking for that humble doer that is willing

38

to serve without seeking some kind of vain glory. Bring Him something; your mind, your heart, or a willingness to support a work of His that is taking place in the earth. Hence, the re-establishment of a Jewish Christian Council back in the heart of Jerusalem. The Bible calls it being workers together with God, an interaction which is designed to create a fire in us by way of His Holy Spirit. This union teaches us to walk in faith and favor and to co-operate with God. He operates in favor when we op-erate in faith. Abraham felt as though he belonged because God gave him the opportunity to co-operate, (to operate in union). The moment that Abraham laid out his offering, the scripture tells us that the fowls came down upon the carcasses, and that Abraham drove them away. Abraham had decided that al-though they were ignorant to what was going on between him and God, as many are, there are some who will oppose us and not even know why, simply because tradition says they should. In Abraham's case, the actions of the fowls were in direct op-position to what God and Abraham had agreed upon. He there-fore made a decision to protect that which he had covenanted to offer up to God. God could have intervened but he didn't, it was Abraham's job to stand in defense of that which he knew was his. When it comes to establishing and keeping covenant with God, there are some things that we cannot do, like keep-ing Israel's enemies from coming against her. Those things we must leave up to Him believing by faith that He will do them. However, no matter how He (God) might choose to move, our hearts must still be directed towards Him. Knowing that what may appear to be a delay or denial on God's part is in fact a call to worship, which is something that we certainly can do.

Faith is an action word, because believing is something that God expects to be done. What if Abraham had decided that there was no need to continue with his sacrifice, because the buzzards were going to get it anyway, because trouble was go-ing to come against it, because challenges were going to rise? What would he have accomplished with an attitude of defeat;

absolutely nothing. It is a known fact that opposition will be lurking around somewhere looking for a favorable opportunity to attack, and try to force us to abort our mission. But, Israel is no stranger to distress, anguish and travail.

"And he said unto Abram, Know of a surety that thy seed shall be a stranger in a land that is not theirs, and shall serve them; and they shall afflict them four hundred years; And also that nation, whom they shall serve, will I judge: and afterward shall they come out with great substance."

Genesis 15:13-14

Here in Genesis God forewarns Abraham of a time when his seed would go into Egyptian captivity. He also assures him that after four hundred years, He would judge that nation which persecuted them. When the time for their deliverance had come, the Israelites or Hebrews would emerge from that captivity with great substance. This is how God explained it to Moses.

"And the Lord said, I have surely seen the affliction of my people which are in Egypt, and have heard their cry by reason of their taskmasters; for I know their sorrows; And I am come down to deliver them out of the hand of the Egyptians, and to bring them up out of that land unto a good land and a large, unto a land flowing with milk and honey; unto the place of the Canaanites, and the Hittites, and the Amorites, and the Perizzites, and the Hivites, and the Jebusites."

Exodus 3:7-8

God's desire for worship had been consummated. Israel's cries unto Him caused Jehovah Shalom (Lord of Peace) to move into action on their behalf.

Israel's deliverance is not a chronicle of their being rescued by hoards of outside sword swinging, super human warriors. It does not resemble the reckless abandon of a heroic world such as the Greeks, Moslems and other ancient people saw as their original state. Stories of Abraham, Isaac, Jacob, Joseph and even Moses are permeated by a sense of divine destiny. They also contain a much simpler, earthly law and tradition. A tradition that reflects a recognizable way of human life in which combat and cunning are replaced with gentler affections of a close knit family. Always when looking back, the Hebrew Nation saw its ancestors as having two main virtues: (1) goodness and an attitude of resolve in human relations; and (2) utter resignation beyond mere humility to accept divine will. Both Christians and Moslem traditions accept the historical authenticity of Abraham and regard him as their spiritual ancestor. But to the Jews, he is the first and unique patriot, the model of Hebrew excellence inspired by his covenant, and woven together by the memories of three generations descended from his loins.

The emergence of this faith had been accurately described as a revolution in the world view of man. All previous and contemporary religions saw human destiny as subject to the laws of nature. Just as the natural cycles returned to their point of origin having no real purpose, so was human life conceived as an endless possession; passing through birth and chaos. Eventually ending once again in the same darkness and chaos from which it came. The gods themselves were subject to human passion, incest and lust. They were associated with natural origins and energies, such as sun, light, air, and fertility. Natural forces were numerous and so were these gods. There was a god for each force at the point of chaos.

The Jew and the Christian however, have received a sense of belonging or nurturing that is unprecedented or unmatched throughout history. This knowledge is essential in our quest to occupy, make our presence known until our Lord returns. Therefore, for us, quitting is not an option. As a result of frustration, intimidation and despair, many a pilgrim have turned and walked away abandoning the faith, leaving in its place a pile of rubble made up of dreams, ideas and promises that may never be realized. So often the question still remains why would God allow evil to exist? The first thing we must understand is that with God every round goes higher. Earlier in this book, we have had the opportunity to take a look at this huge canvas upon which God has not yet completed His masterpiece. If you have ever decorated a Christmas tree or watch someone else do so, you will notice that with all the beautiful ornaments, all the beautiful lights, it's still not complete until it is crowned with the star. God is building something, he is working on something that is eternal in nature, and we are all part of that work in progress. We must learn to see a bigger picture, a picture of which you and I have a part, a picture much bigger than anything that we will have to face in this world. It's not about suffering. It's not even about living or dying, it's all about divine design. Any part of us that we exercise the most will become the strongest part.

Therefore, those individuals who exercise hatred, racial prejudice, oppression, betrayal and vile affection will become strong in those areas. But, we are told to exercise our faith through praise, prayer, worship and love. The Apostle Paul was a shining example of this.

"I have planted, Apollos watered; but God gave the increase."
I Corinthians 3:6

Both Paul and Apollos became living sacrifices unto God, in that they had given their entire lives for the work of the ministry. As a result of their sacrifice, God gave them increase. No matter what one might be going through or how bad things may appear to be, we must remember that its only a stepping stone to greater things, and if we continue to trust and worship God, its only one way we can go and that is upward, higher into heavenly places.

"Therefore leaving the principles of the doctrine of Christ, let us go on unto perfection; not laying again the foundation of repentance from dead works, and of faith toward God."
Hebrews 6:1

Paul was an adventurer who knew God in a way that most men had not known Him, and for this reason he would not allow himself to be hemmed in by traditions established by men, even those of his own company. Paul was concerned that the Church would find itself going around in circles instead of forging ahead towards the greatness that was assigned to it. Paul understood that through the blood of Christ, by faith, that he was tied to something that was bigger than life. He refused to let anyone make little of that fact. Just listen to this statement with your heart in light of some of the things I have already shared with you.

"For we know that the whole creation groaneth and travaileth in pain together until now."
Romans 8:22

Here the creature is groaning deep within itself to become one once again with all creation. Paul calls it the adoption of the sons of God, both Jew and Gentile being grafted into the universal family, and this without a doubt will be a crowning moment.

"Beloved, now are we the sons of God, and it doth not yet appear what we shall be: but we know that, when he shall appear, we shall be like him; for we shall see him as he is."
1 John 3:2

If you are a believer, this should surely stir your imagination and cause you to wonder, what this could be like.

"But as it is written, Eye hath not seen, nor ear heard, neither have entered into the heart of man, the things which God hath prepared for them that love him."

1 Corinthians 2:9

This scripture and all that it encompasses certainly sheds light on the hymn that says:

> Amazing grace how sweet the sound;
>   that saved a wretch like me.
>
> I once was lost, but now I'm found;
>   was blind, but now I see.

What a wonderful blessing it is when God allows one to be able to see beyond the trials of their natural surroundings, and be able to call Him from those places of despair. Allowing us to understand His motives and share with others His magnificent plan of salvation, a plan which includes the coming together of both Jews and Gentiles in His Church. As we answer this exciting call to worship, it incites us to begin again in Jerusalem, for this is truly the next level of progression for those who are called the Sons of God.

Chapter 5

Zion's View

"By the rivers of Babylon, there we sat down, yea, we wept, when we remembered Zion. We hanged our harps upon the willows in the midst thereof. For there they that carried us away captive required of us a song; and they that wasted us required of us mirth, saying, Sing us one of the songs of Zion. How shall we sing the LORD's song in a strange land? If I forget thee, O Jerusalem, let my right hand forget her cunning. If I do not remember thee, let my tongue cleave to the roof of my mouth; if I prefer not Jerusalem above my chief joy."

Psalms 137:1-6 KJV

"But ye are a chosen generation, a royal priesthood, an holy nation, a peculiar people; that ye should shew forth the praises of him who hath called you out of darkness into his marvellous light: Which in time past were not a people, but are now the people of God: which had not obtained mercy, but now have obtained mercy."

1Peter 2:9-10 KJV

In both these literary movements there is an air of poetic splendor, grace and acceptance. The resolve that emanates from these voices of the past speaks directly to the heart of all that is loved, shared and reverenced by an ensemble of people, who openly acknowledge the favor of God upon their lives. One is by divine birth right; the other has been grafted in according to the election of grace. Israel, the chosen people, is lamenting as though a huge door had been slammed shut against them, separating them from their divine heritage. "How can we sing the songs of Zion in a strange land?" And the Church, the chosen generation who believed that a huge door had been opened to them as a direct result of this audacious, defiant new covenant that was initiated by Jesus on Calvary... "a people who were not a people, but who have now become people of God."

Both these groups collectively make up a select remnant of believers that God is assembling at this crucial juncture of the

Judeo-Christian legacy. It all began to change in 1948, when Israel's door to God's promises was reopened. She was widely accepted by much of the world as a sovereign nation. For the Jews, this was a moment that was way overdue. A moment that they felt had been purchased by the blood, sweat, and tears of millions of their fellow laborers. From this agonizing reminiscence, a phrase was infused to symbolize a well deserved independence of a determined people. The phrase affectionately embraced was "NEVER AGAIN."

"So shall my word be that goeth forth out of my mouth: it shall not return unto me void, but it shall accomplish that which I please, and it shall prosper in the thing whereto I sent it. For ye shall go out with joy, and be led forth with peace: the mountains and the hills shall break forth before you into singing, and all the trees of the field shall clap their hands. Instead of the thorn shall come up the fir tree, and instead of the brier shall come up the myrtle tree: and it shall be to the LORD for a name, for an everlasting sign that shall not be cut off."
Isaiah 55:11-13 KJV

Immediately after the formation of what was called the State of Israel, the Jewish people began to reach out in all directions for their brothers and sisters that had been exiled from their homeland for far too long. In the winters of 1948 and 1949 the camps in Cyprus where the British had held thousands of Jews were finally closed. Israeli forces seized an Egyptian stronghold in Beersheba later Galilee, and old communities of Yemen and Iraq where Jews had lived before Moslems and Arab history had begun. The creation of a Jewish state was like the sound of a trumpet, calling them to change the direction of their lives and to join the construction of a new society.

Operation Magic Carpet lifted thousands of Midianite Jews to Israel, the last of them in September 1950. As with most sovereign countries there are three main factors that constitute the staples of commitment to the people of that nation: security, economics and progress. To date, Israel's military is one of the most formidable in the modern world. It's Army, Air Force and Navy are all well manned and ready to move at a moment's notice. After 1956, the next ten years proved to be the most fertile progression in Israel's history. Israel prospered, the economy flourished, immigration had increased and her international position had broadened year by year. Ninety-one Israeli embassies existed in all the five continents of the world. None of these accomplishments however, came without great cost. The Jews paid dearly for every inch of ground they recovered. That's why in order to ensure continued progress; Israel's leaders must use sound judgment in determining who her real allies are. ZION'S VIEW must enable her to recognize essential strategies that should be set in motion for the greater good. This would require a sincere collaboration with some who presently might exist outside of her normal, social or religious parameters. Of course, before such an arrangement could be taken seriously, there would first have to be a considerable amount of trust. Trust is a strong reliance, confidence, and belief which is formulated when one party or group is convinced that others understand their hopes, dreams, ideas, concerns, and values. They will never violate them. Mutual trust is when the other party believes that they can expect the same thing in return. As far as having something in common is concerned, for the most part, both Jew and Christian have been persecuted and are now being threatened by the same enemies.

"And who is he that will harm you, if ye be followers of that which is good? But and if ye suffer for righteousness' sake, happy are ye: and be not afraid of their terror, neither be troubled; But sanctify the Lord God in your hearts: and be ready always to give an answer to every man that asketh you a reason of the hope that is in you with meekness and fear."

1Peter 3:13-15 KJV

This epistle was written by a Jewish brother who was operating under a dangerous set of circumstances. He was trying to promote an unpopular doctrine. Many of his company had already been placed in prison or worst. Yet under heavy persecution, he still found it within himself to encourage or remind those who remained true to their convictions, that because they were on the side of good they should not be afraid. Therefore, he wrote, be ready always to give an answer to every man that asks you a reason of the hope that is within you. Not in a brazen high-minded kind of way, but in meekness and fear.

We understand Zion's View, that's why we are called "Infidels" by those who have sworn to destroy us both. At least in that regard, and in the interest of taking action for the greater good, it is essential that we unite our efforts against those who are rapidly mounting their efforts against us. Our assignment is to step out on that which we know to be right, to submerge ourselves into the things that we preach, because the action of the witness is more compelling than the words that proceed out of their mouths. As the chosen generation our primary goal is to set an agenda against anti-Semitism and to advocate the rebirth of the Jerusalem Counsel in Jerusalem. We know in large part it is because of this ungodly conspiracy, that the Church and the Jewish Nation continue to remain divided.

"Pray for the peace of Jerusalem: they shall prosper that love thee."

Psalm 122:6 KJV

This passage substantiates our assertion that Israel is God's gift to the world. *"They shall prosper that love thee."* God has set in place a directive which will foster dialogue culminating into tremendous blessings for those who love both Israel and the Church. This is not just an opportunity that God is offering a few enlightened people; this is a mandate for the entire body of Christ. It is imperative for the greater good of Israel that Jew and Gentile Christians learn to trust each other. As we move forward we must be willing to confront those things that might abate our progress or confuse our primary objective. For the greater good of Israel, we must pray for wisdom and honesty within our ranks knowing that our first challenge, will be finding ways to confront the prejudices and suspicions that are mostly born out of tradition, and maintained by a sense of loyalty to those who have passed them on to us.

"Now I beseech you, brethren, by the name of our Lord Jesus Christ, that ye all speak the same thing, and that there be no divisions among you; but that ye be perfectly joined together in the same mind and in the same judgment."

1 Corinthians 1:10 KJV

Here, the writer Paul is dealing with what I'm going to term learned behavior. He has a group of people from diverse backgrounds who have different opinions, attitudes, and ideas about how a certain thing should be approached. So as not to appear intrusive or to belittle their way of reasoning, he begins by saying; I employ you brethren in the name of Him who we all trust, and for the sake of the greater good, that we seek common ground.

"For, brethren, ye have been called unto liberty; only use not liberty for an occasion to the flesh, but by love serve one another."

Galatians 5:13 KJV

Here again, the Apostle Paul is called to open the heart of God to the Gentiles. He is addressing people who knew all too well what it was like to live under tyranny, shame and oppression. His inference here is that too often those who have been set free from physical, emotional or mental imprisonment will have a tendency to want to celebrate. The problem is that the only example of celebration was that which they had learned

50

by observing their former captors. It's never a good idea to try and imitate those who might see you as not being equal. Paul informs them that they had been "called to liberty." This meant that their freedom did not come as a result of a change of heart of their oppressors, but as a result of a supernatural decree from an unseen power. This is a force greater than anyone could obstruct; Him whom we worship, God. Paul informs us that there is no room for vain glory or selfish intent. We must learn to channel our enthusiasm through the corridors of *love* with a commitment to serve. It's in that same spirit, that we must present ourselves to our beloved companion Israel. To build her confidence that as the Church, we not only understand, but that we are also determined to protect Zion's view.

Chapter 6

An Ensign to the Nations

"And he shall set up an ensign for the nations, and shall assemble the outcasts of Israel, and gather together the dispersed of Judah from the four corners of the earth."

Isaiah 11:12 KJV

In our previous chapter we talked about Zion's view. However, over and again God has made it emphatically clear, that His view of us and our view of ourselves are often miles apart. Webster defines ensign as a flag, banner or symbol of authority. There is a sense however, that no nation with the kind of humble and unassuming history as Israel has had, would be interested in carrying that kind of a banner or responsibility. No matter how much favor it might afford her. Just think Jerusalem is not only the heart and soul of Judaism but, is also the birthplace, center and stronghold of the Christian Church. Now that's authority with a capital A for Amen. Just as the work that God is performing upon most of mankind and the world in general, has yet to be completed, God's work in, around and through the Nation of Israel is also still a work in progress.

It's apparent that God has a plan for Israel that goes beyond her ability to totally comprehend, but the fact still remains that through all of her ups and downs God has never taken his eyes off of his beloved chosen people. However, this mantle upon Abraham's seed would prove to be both a blessing and a curse. Though God was always with her, for some Jews this is one truth that was sometimes hard to swallow, as down through the centuries Israel's enemies have grown in increasing numbers.

It is not always easy to make the case that you are the sole heirs to a land that was already occupied for generations before you got there. But the scriptures are filled with God's profound response to this human form of inductive reasoning.

"For every beast of the forest is mine, and the cattle upon a thousand hills. I know all the fowls of the mountains: and the wild beasts of the field are mine. If I were hungry, I would not tell thee: for the world is mine, and the fullness thereof."
Psalm 50:10-12 KJV

Though the implementation of God's blue print for Israel's preeminence and renown often seem futile or unavailing, her future as an ensign to the nations was never truly threatened. All through the scriptures we are given prophetic forecast, earmarks and inevitable signals as to how this preconceived movement of God would end up. The prophetic movement is the most original and potent expression of Hebrew thought, and if one would be open to the spirit they would find in abundance glimpses into Israel's future exploits.

Possibly the most celebrated of all of Israel's kings was King David (whose name meant 'beloved'). David certainly held a special place in the heart of God. He was the second king of the United Kingdom of the Hebrew people after King Saul. As a young boy he was the keeper of his father's sheep, and showed a great deal of courage and faithfulness by killing both a lion and a bear which tried to attack the flock. Young David also displayed an outstanding musical talent with the harp, a fact which figured prominently in his life. When Saul was rejected by God as King, the prophet Samuel went to Bethlehem to anoint David as the future king of Israel. David, an ancestor of Jesus Christ and writer of numerous songs, lived a life filled with one adventurous or notable incident after another.

"And David was afraid of God that day, saying, How shall I bring the ark of God home to me? So David brought not the ark home to himself to the city of David, but carried it aside into the house of Obed-edom the Gittite. And the ark of God remained with the family of Obed-edom in his house three

months. And the LORD blessed the house of Obed-edom, and all that he had."

1 Chronicles 13:12-14 KJV

After reading this scripture I received a starling revelation, that in some cases when that which represents the anointing of God is not located at its rightful place, those who are in possession of it can still benefit from His presence. This was indeed an in season revelation, i.e. (the head of the Christian Church not being in Jerusalem but in Rome). Like prophecies, all revelations do not always take place in the season in which they were given. This was certainly a heart wrenching occurrence for David and all Israel. They had finally retrieved from the Philistines the most sacred Ark of the Covenant. This was to represent the presence of God in their midst. It was a brief time of great celebration. The joy and exuberance that these people shared was awe inspiring, as one reads this biblical account of what was to be one of Israel's finest moments. When the cart carrying the Ark reached a certain point, and the oxen stumbled, Uzza put forth his hand to hold the Ark and God took his life. Apparently this man Uzza not being a priest, should have never laid his hands upon that which was most sacred to God.

Being shocked, confused, and afraid to bring the Ark to himself, David instead took it aside to the house of Obed-edom who was possibly one of his body guards. Here is an interesting note; the Bible tells us that although the Ark was not in its proper place (that is to say in Israel's possession) for three months the house of Obed-edom prospered.

The fact that Rome has enjoyed world-wide recognition, and has certainly prospered in an unprecedented way from her statute as the center of the Christian Church, does not mean that her imminence or her religious superiority was to be permanent. Nowhere are we told that God would make Rome an ensign to the Nations, NOWHERE!

"And he shall set up an ensign for the nations, and shall assemble the outcasts of Israel."

Isaiah 11:12 KJV

Just as David and all Israel believed that the very presence of the Ark in their midst was confirmation that God was with them, so do we believe today, that once the Jerusalem Council is returned to its place of origin in Jerusalem, Israel will also stand as our assurance that God is with us.

"Thus all Israel brought up the ark of the covenant of the LORD with shouting, and with sound of the cornet, and with trumpets, and with cymbals, making a noise with psalteries and harps."

1 Chronicles 15:28 KJV

Even though David himself lived in a king's house and wore fine linen, his passion to retrieve the Ark so that *all Israel* could be blessed never faltered.

"But ye shall receive power, after that the Holy Ghost is come upon you: and ye shall be witnesses unto me both in Jerusalem, and in all Judaea, and in Samaria, and unto the uttermost part of the earth."

Acts 1:8 KJV

Using David and all Israel as our example, we should incorporate that same passion and determination in order that we too might recover that which was lost. It is our hope that all Christians, including those of the Roman Catholic Church might see this for what it is; not just a mandate or directive from God, but an opportunity to be witnesses and recipients of the most abundant outpouring of God's presence this generation has ever seen. One filled with power and heightened anticipation of the greatest event that this world has even known - the second coming of our Blessed Messiah and Lord Jesus Christ.

"And the apostles and brethren that were in Judaea heard that the Gentiles had also received the word of God. And when Peter was come up to Jerusalem, they that were of the circumcision contended with him, Saying, Thou wentest in to men uncircumcised, and didst eat with them."

Acts 11:1-3 KJV

This scripture goes on to tell us that the Apostle Peter, a Jew, rehearsed this same matter with the Jerusalem counsel and expounded it by order. He explained to them what had happened, and why he had conducted himself in the manner that he did.

We must be willing to reach out to those who are currently undecided about the future direction of their lives and of the Church. Be it the corporate executive, the man next door or the broken and disenfranchised brother or sister on the street. We must let them know that all the barriers, challenges, false starts and missteps that appear to be persistent in making life meaningless, can and will be confronted in a new way. We now have access to the formula for blessings. Our returning to the pattern that God have set in place before the foundation of the world. Just as the Ark stood as an ensign to David and all Israel, so shall the reestablishment of the Jerusalem Counsel stand as an ensign to all who would believe, so that we might aid Israel in fulfilling her destiny as an ensign, banner, and symbol of reconciliation to the entire world.

Chapter 7

An Engaging Destiny

"His foundation is in the holy mountains. The Lord loveth the gates of Zion more than all the dwellings of Jacob. Glorious things are spoken of thee, O city of God. Selah."
Psalms 87:1-3 KJV

The term engaging is defined as winning, enchanting, captivating, disarming and lovable. That's why this short Psalm classified as a Song of Zion is one of the most engaging in the entire collection of Psalms. On the one hand, it is remarkably brief and to the point; almost to the place of being hidden or unnoticed. While on the other, it's deep seated love for Jerusalem is equaled to that expressed in **Psalms 137:5-6;** *"If I forget thee, O Jerusalem, let my right hand forget her cunning, If I do not remember thee, let my tongue cleave to the roof of my mouth; if I prefer not Jerusalem above my chief joy."* KJV

In Psalms 87 a Hebrew has his foundation, his purpose, his entire being couched or entrenched in the holy mountains. The gates and the marketplaces are the center of economic and social life of Jerusalem. Here in Scripture, the gates also represent the whole city; a city that God loves even more than the dwelling places of Jacob, which is any place where Israelites reside. The glorious things that the psalmist may have had in mind are:

a. The Lord has chosen Zion for his habitation (Psalms 132:13)
b. That Holy Mountain, beautiful in elevation is the joy of all the earth. (Psalms 48:2)
c. And many people shall go and say, Come ye, and let us go up to the mountain of the Lord, to the house of the God of Jacob; and he will teach us of his ways, and we will walk in his paths: for out of Zion shall go forth the law, and the word of the Lord from Jerusalem. (Isaiah 2:3)

Here the eagle eyed Prophet has seen the global influence of the Jerusalem Council.

". . . O habitation of justice, and mountain of holiness."
Jeremiah 31:23b KJV

All of these glorious things are spoken of the city of God. The first and most obvious glory of the city is geographical. It was built on a mountainous pedestal from which it dominated the world, and to which it drew the eyes of the nations of the earth.

"Ye are the light of the world. A city that is set on an hill cannot be hid."
Matthew 5:14 KJV

"By faith Abraham, when he was called to go out into a place which he should after receive for an inheritance, obeyed; and he went out, not knowing whither he went. By faith he sojourned in the land of promise, as in a strange country, dwelling in tabernacles with Isaac and Jacob, the heirs with him of the same promise: For he looked for a city which hath foundations, whose builder and maker is God.
Hebrews 11:8-10 KJV

These were the engaging things spoken about Zion, and glorious indeed they were. It is hard to imagine one having these kinds of deep seated affections for their native land, and it not be reflected in their lives on a daily basis. Even if they were not physically present, or had been forced into exile; which might be the case with most of the Church and definitely the case of the Jerusalem Council. Out of humble beginnings is greatness spawned, I don't know if anyone has ever made this assertion before, but it sounded good to me and so I have said it. Just as a matter of observation, Israel's destiny seems to have had a mind all of its own. Even when the people didn't know who they were, or where they were headed, prosperity followed them wherever they went. When Israel entered Canaan, she was not a nation. Her formative years still lay ahead of her. The transitions from a semi-migratory or wandering people to an agricultural society, the transformation from tribe to nation were all influenced by contact with the populations of Canaan.

There must have been periods of peaceful relations among the Israelites and Canaanites, because we know that a merging of cultures took place. The Israelites settled among a civilization higher than their own. But it was as though this mysterious ambiance surrounded them and directed their every move.

"The angel of the Lord encampeth round about them that fear him, and delivereth them."

Psalm 34:7 KJV

The material condition of the Israelites slowly improved. They became a nation of small farmers. They learned to build artificial reservoirs and underground tanks for storing water for use during dry seasons. In dire need for more soil they showed resourcefulness and reclaimed land from deserts and forests. Their towns few and badly fortified were more of the pasture or rural nature, unlike the strongholds of the Canaanites and Philistines. Israel's strength depended on the number of men under arms who could be mustered in case of need. More often than not, tribal law was perceived to have prevailed against Israel's larger or greater interest.

"In those days there was no king in Israel, but every man did that which was right in his own eyes."

Judges 17:6 KJV

Two centuries, (1230 BC-1030 BC) divide the conquest of Canaan from the reign of Israel's first King, Saul. There were no political groups or heads of state to issue directives on how the country should be governed, or what direction it should take. These were known as the days when Judges ruled. In times of crisis, the people would make their appeal to the Judges who were the overseers of the public's interest.

Even before the Judges, Abraham and his nephew Lot showed examples of inner tribal conflict. They were all of one clan but had different herdsmen who disputed over land and water rights. Abraham desiring to put an end to the discord gave Lot the right of first choice.

"Then Lot chose him all the plain of Jordan; and Lot journeyed east: and they separated themselves the one from the other. Abram dwelled in the land of Canaan, and Lot dwelled in the cities of the plain, and pitched his tent toward Sodom."
Genesis 13:11-12 KJV

Because of the loss of Lot, Abraham feared even more that God could not keep his promises concerning His seed, and so Sarah his wife got involved, and followed the local customs. Sarah asked Abraham to sleep with her maid Hagar, but once Hagar conceived, Sarah drove her out into the desert.

"And the angel of the LORD said unto her, Return to thy mistress, and submit thyself under her hands. And the angel of the LORD said unto her, I will multiply thy seed exceedingly, that it shall not be numbered for multitude. And the angel of the LORD said unto her, Behold, thou art with child, and shalt bear a son, and shalt call his name Ishmael; because the LORD hath heard thy affliction. And he will be a wild man; his hand will be against every man, and every man's hand against him; and he shall dwell in the presence of all his brethren."
Genesis 16:9-12 KJV

After her encounter with the Angel, Hagar returned to Abraham's household and had her son whom she named Ishmael, and he would become the father of the Moslem Nation.

Later while living at a place called Mamre, three strangers visited Abraham and astonished him. They told him that his wife Sarah who was old and never bore children would soon have a son. Abraham believed the strangers and a year later Sarah gave birth to a boy child whose name was to be Isaac.

For a time Abraham did what many of us have done; he allowed his circumstances to dictate his actions. Instead of seeing through the eye of promise, he saw only through the eye of circumstance. From the loins of Abraham Ishmael became the son of circumstance, an offspring of the situation. Isaac however, became the son of promise and the offspring of faith. Who would have guessed, that both these children who were Abraham's sons, would one day make a lasting impression on the entire human population. Later Abraham's faith was tested a second time, when God asked him to sacrifice Isaac the promised child, back to him. By faith Abraham proceeded to follow God's instructions without question. However, at the very last moment God provided Himself with another sacrifice, a ram caught in the bush. This was all done so that Isaac and his seed might be saved by the shedding of blood.

After this confirmation of Abraham's faith and obedience, God affirmed his covenant with him, promising Abraham again many descendents, and that through him all Nations would be blessed. Abraham's faith and acceptance of God's terms established the first covenant between the Jewish people and their God. Keeping with His covenant, these words were spoken to Moses during the Hebrews wilderness experience.

"And his miracles, and his acts, which he did in the midst of Egypt unto Pharaoh the king of Egypt, and unto all his land;

And what he did unto the army of Egypt, unto their horses, and to their chariots; how he made the water of the Red sea to overflow them as they pursued after you, and how the LORD hath destroyed them unto this day; And what he did unto you in the wilderness, until ye came into this place."

Deuteronomy 11:3-5

"Therefore shall ye keep all the commandments which I command you this day, that ye may be strong, and go in and possess the land, whither ye go to possess it; And that ye may prolong your days in the land, which the LORD sware unto your fathers to give unto them and to their seed, a land that floweth with milk and honey. For the land, whither thou goest in to possess it, is not as the land of Egypt, from whence ye came out, where thou sowedst thy seed, and wateredst it with thy foot, as a garden of herbs: But the land, whither ye go to possess it, is a land of hills and valleys, and drinketh water of the rain of heaven: A land which the LORD thy God careth for: the eyes of the LORD thy God are always upon it, from the beginning of the year even unto the end of the year."

Deuteronomy 11:8-12. KJV

This narrative from Deuteronomy refers to the land known since the 5th Century as Palestine. This area is also similarly referred to in whole or part as the Holy Land, the Promise Land, Canaan, Judah, or Judea, and Israel. Beyond its special place in Israel's history, the exodus was to become an engaging symbol preserving the idea of social liberation around the world. The words of Henry George, "from between the paws of the rock heavy sphinx rises the genius of human liberty and the trumpets of the exodus throb with the divine proclamation of the rights of man."

Benjamin Franklin and Thomas Jefferson when consulted on the emblem of the future American union, they suggested that the seal of the United States should represent the children of Israel, fleeing across the parted waters of the Red Sea on their way to freedom. This portrayal gave rise to the slogan; "Resistance to tyrants is obedience to God."

At the national convention of revolutionary France, popular leaders spoke of themselves as inheritors of the "new Canaan". Whether they saw liberation from a foreign yoke or from degradation or poverty, men were to use the images of the exodus to symbolize a possibility of swift transition from servitude to freedom, from darkness to light. Herein lies historical literary proof, that when it comes down to Israel having an engaging destiny, even the exodus would loom as a shining example of mankind's determination to be free. It would have a continued impact on the thoughts, attitudes and actions of men of every Nation, creed, race and color. The exodus as a constant reminder echoes in many times and distant lands the engaging idea of a people and their God doing great exploits together.

Chapter 8

When God is Not Enough

"And the Lord spake unto Moses that selfsame day, saying, Get thee up into this mountain Abarim, unto mount Nebo, which is in the land of Moab, that is over against Jericho; and behold the land of Canaan, which I give unto the children of Israel for a possession: And die in the mount whither thou goest up, and be gathered unto thy people; as Aaron thy brother died in mount Hor, and was gathered unto his people."

Deuteronomy 32:48-50 KJV

This passage in Deuteronomy heralds the close of one era and the beginning of another. Moses had served out his duration as prophet, deliverer, leader and law giver of the Hebrew people. During his period as a leader, Moses was so inspired by God, that he was able to build a united nation among a race of oppressed and weary slaves. But Moses would eventually succumb to the wants and desires of his people, rather than the desires of God. It had become evident to Moses at this point in their pilgrimage that their faith was waning and for some overtly trusting in God was not enough. At the close of this movement, Moses had only one more task to fulfill before ascending up Mount Nebo where he would take his last breath. His final assignment was to bless the children of Israel. He would then gaze over into a land flowing with milk and honey for the first and last time, a land that he himself would not be allowed to enter; this land was called Canaan. Under the leadership of Moses the Hebrews had endured an arduous journey through the desert to reach Canaan. It was here that the first kings - Saul, David and Solomon created the Kingdom of Israel.

This land remained of fundamental importance to its people throughout its subsequent history. Its division into rival kingdoms of Israel and Judah, their fall to the Assyrians and Babylonians, the exile of the people of Judah and their return to the land ruled successively by Persia, Greece and Rome.

"Then all the elders of Israel gathered themselves together, and came to Samuel unto Ramah, And said unto him, Behold, thou art old, and thy sons walk not in thy ways: now make us a king to judge us like all the nations."

1 Samuel 8:4-5 KJV

It is a forgone conclusion that God is never slack concerning His promises. It's only when we set out to take matters into our own hands, do we often end up digging a hole for ourselves which only He can get us out of.

"And the Lord said unto Samuel, Hearken unto the voice of the people in all that they say unto thee: for they have not rejected thee, but they have rejected me, that I should not reign over them."

1Samuel 8:7 KJV

The people had made up their minds that they no longer wanted to serve this invisible God, they wanted someone they could see, touch and hear an audible voice. They wanted a man who could sit tall on a horse and go before them in battle. Samuel the last Judge of Israel, tried to warn them of the consequences of having a man rather than the God that delivered them out of Egypt to reign over them. We must be careful not to get too comfortable with the idea of setting one man over all the affairs of the entire Church. However, these people were adamant their minds were made up because this is what happens to men when God is not enough.

"Nevertheless the people refused to obey the voice of Samuel; and they said, Nay; but we will have a king over us; That we also may be like all the nations; and that our king may judge us, and go out before us, and fight our battles."

1 Samuel 8:19-20 KJV

They had forgotten what it was like to draw breath and thrive under the protection of God's Shekinah Glory. They had also forgotten about those times when they would lift Him up in praise, how they themselves would be lifted up above the frightful, and threatening demands that so often confronted them.

Let me make it clear, that this observation is in no way intended to level an indictment against the people of God. I believe that at its core, Israel loved God, but like so many before and after her they were unable to relinquish their will for His. This left them juggling loyalties and trying to glean the best of both worlds... the world of righteous Judaism under the Law of Moses, and the world of the uncircumcised Gentiles that was filled with folly, kings and idols.

"Whoso despiseth the word shall be destroyed: but he that feareth the commandment shall be rewarded. The law of the wise is a fountain of life, to depart from the snares of death."
Proverbs 13:13-14 KJV

This Proverb was written by King Solomon, the king who acquired the reputation of being the wisest man that ever lived. Following the death of Solomon and the ensuing division of the kingdom, Israel on the north and Judah on the south, Israel's link to Jerusalem was broken. A duality of military campaigns against them ensued, first by the Assyrians in 732 B.C. As the empire of the Assyrians declined, its powerful east rival Babylon grew in strength. The kingdom of Judah was caught in the struggle of the two, and Egypt's attempts to intervene. The Babylonians defeated the Assyrians, drove out the Egyptians and created a vast new empire. They twice invaded Judah and annexing the Israelite kingdom. After the attack of Jerusalem in 586 B.C., they carried off its leading citizens into exile in Babylon. The destruction of Jerusalem and its temple by the Babylonians, and the enforced journey into Babylon of the exiled Jews, left them feeling that they had been abandoned by God.

However, the prophets Jeremiah and Ezekiel assured them that they, God's children, would eventually return with renewed faith to the promise land. This guarantee would be repeated over and over again by reminding them that no matter what men might do to them, the land, Israel's land would always be there. Later God would call into service a Persian King by the name of Cyrus the Great. In 539 B.C., Cyrus conquered Babylon bringing Judah under Persian control. The empire created when Cyrus captured territory from the Medes, the Lydians, and Babylonians would not be surpassed until the time of Alexander the Great. Cyrus the Great built up his vast empire on a combination of military might and religious tolerance. Cyrus sent many Jews exiled in Babylon back to Judah. This policy was continued in the next century under Artaxerxes, one of Cyrus' successors. This wave would lead in the true refounding of the Jewish Nation under the leadership of Nehemiah and Ezra. Nehemiah, a servant in the king's court had the King's ear. When Nehemiah expressed concern for his homeland and the fact that the city was in ruins, Artaxerxes decided to appoint him governor of Ahud, a Persian province which was in fact Judah.

King Artaxerxes would send Nehemiah under escort back to the province with instructions to rebuild the city. On the other hand, Ezra was a priest rather than a political leader. If Nehemiah was responsible for the rebuilding the city of Jerusalem, then to Ezra fell the task of reviving Judaism.

The whole account of Israel's history up to this point is in fact a testament of God's faithfulness to his blood covenants. Whatever God signs in blood will remain intact no matter what the party or parties on the other side of the agreement might do.

This chapter was not written to highlight the downside of human nature or man's inability to work in union with God. On the contrary, it is to place a strong emphasis on God's determination to work in union with man, to prove that when it comes to meeting our needs He is more than adequate.

"Not that we are sufficient of ourselves to think any thing as of ourselves; but our sufficiency is of God."

II Corinthians 3:5 KJV

Once God has decreed a certain thing, it's never a matter of if, but with Him it's simply a matter of when. We know that there are many who promote the doctrine of abandonment by the inference that God bailed out on Israel when they needed Him most. They continue to fan the flame by asking the question, what happened to the covenant that promised prosperity and protection? The events of Israel's past clearly show that God like a devout father, even when His children were oblivious to His motives, was always teaching. The lesson that was to be learned is how easily we can fall prey to the aggressions of our enemies or adversaries, when Him whom we worship - God is not enough.

Chapter 9

A New Covenant

"Behold, the days come, saith the LORD, that I will make a new covenant with the house of Israel, and with the house of Judah: Not according to the covenant that I made with their fathers in the day that I took them by the hand to bring them out of the land of Egypt; which my covenant they brake, although I was an husband unto them, saith the LORD: But this shall be the covenant that I will make with the house of Israel; After those days, saith the LORD, I will put my law in their inward parts, and write it in their hearts; and will be their God, and they shall be my people. And they shall teach no more every man his neighbour, and every man his brother, saying, Know the LORD: for they shall all know me, from the least of them unto the greatest of them, saith the LORD: for I will forgive their iniquity, and I will remember their sin no more."

Jeremiah 31:31-34 KJV

Through the Jewish prophet Jeremiah, God informs us of a new covenant that would be introduced in detail at a later time, "Behold the day's come." This new covenant fixed in God's mind and purposed in His heart, would be based solely on the counsel of His own will. In other words, the operative statement in Jeremiah's prophecy is, "I will make a new"... there were no votes cast or opinions sought after concerning His decision. After reading Jeremiah's prophecy, one is left with the notion that this expansive plan would extend beyond the boundaries of race, creed or color -"for they shall all know me." This makes perfectly good sense when we consider the fact that if there is but one God, a belief shared by Jews, Christians and Islamic alike, then He would have to be the one and only creator of all mankind. This would also mean that everyone was included in his plan, and would therefore have some specific role to fulfill. It is imperative that we begin to take a look at both our selective and collective roles, and prepare ourselves to boldly step into them.

"Behold, I will send my messenger, and he shall prepare the way before me: and the LORD, whom ye seek, shall suddenly come to his temple, even the messenger of the covenant, whom ye delight in: behold, he shall come, saith the LORD of hosts."

Malachi 3:1 KJV

Once again God is speaking to us, this time by the prophet Malachi. He promises to send His messenger John the Baptist, who would be the front runner of Jesus Christ; another extremely confident and equally impressive messenger and interpreter of the New Covenant. It would be four hundred years between the close of the Old Testament with Malachi as its last prophet, and the opening of the Christian or "Common Era" with Matthew. These would be known by many as the "silent years", as there appeared to be no open vision from God.

From the re-founding of the nation under Persian rule with Nehemiah and Ezra, (444 B.C.E.), to the savage overthrow of Jerusalem the Judean capital, by the Roman general Pompeii, there was an extremely powerful Jewish enthusiasm among the inhabitants of Judah. Always there seemed to be this sense of a new day with brand new possibilities for Judah's independence. It created a strong belief that this independence loomed just around the corner. At the birth of Christianity, the Jewish presence had already crossed the boundaries of Palestine. Jews had settled in almost all the countries in the civilized world. The name Palestine entered common usage during the Greco-Roman period, a period influenced by both Greeks and Romans. In the Bible it was used to designate the country of the Philistines, a coastal stretch adjoining the Sharon valley. The Romans conquering the land in 63 B.C.E. took the name of the province of Judah to be the whole of the land.

The Tulmud (a collection of Jewish, civil and religious laws) in referring to Palestine speaks of it simply as the land; a term which has endured in Jewish terminology to this day. The province basked in the great distinction of Jerusalem and the temple. The whole Diaspora looked upon it as the center of the world. Jerusalem's population estimated at 120,000 was at times swollen by masses of pilgrims, who periodically outnumbered the local population. The temple and the court provided permanent employment. Jerusalem was the seat of the High Priest and the Sanhedrin, in which rich land owners, well to do merchants and craftsmen, found it attractive for settlement. There was a thriving business in luxuries, including precious stones and expensive cloth. But for the residents of Galilee it was different. Their region was the main center of the common people. There were no great centers of learning and boasted no large cities or famous teachings. Its inhabitants could not compare in scholarship with the population that lived close to the splendor of the temple. Many dispossessed and landless could be found wondering from village to village. From these downtrodden Jews came Jesus of Nazareth.

"The day following Jesus would go forth into Galilee, and findeth Philip, and saith unto him, Follow me. Now Philip was of Bethsaida, the city of Andrew and Peter. Philip findeth Nathanael, and saith unto him, We have found him, of whom Moses in the law, and the prophets, did write, Jesus of Nazareth, the son of Joseph. And Nathanael said unto him, Can there any good thing come out of Nazareth? Philip saith unto him, Come and see".

John 1:43-46 KJV

Many agreed that if there was a time when they needed a deliverer in the likeness of Moses it was then. However things were different, they were already located in the land of promise, so they did not have to be physically drawn out of a particular place, but rather drawn in spiritually and introduced to a whole new way of thinking; a new kingdom in which they would be regarded as prominent citizens – even as kings and princesses.

"And when he was demanded of the Pharisees, when the king-dom of God should come, he answered them and said, The king-dom of God cometh not with observation: Neither shall they say, Lo here! or, lo there! for, behold, the kingdom of God is within you."
Luke 17:20-21 KJV

This kind of language was offensive to some of the religious leaders of that era. They could not get their minds around or come to grips with the idea, that a man who did not concur with their schools of thought, who had not set under the tutelage of the priesthood, would dare try and pass himself off as some new religious leader of the disenfranchised; both Jew and Gentile. And if that was not enough, this man Jesus also claimed to be "the Son of God."

"Jesus answered them, Many good works have I shewed you from my Father; for which of those works do ye stone me? The Jews answered him, saying, For a good work we stone thee not; but for blasphemy; and because that thou, being a man, makest thyself God. Jesus answered them, Is it not written in your law, I said, Ye are gods? If he called them gods, unto whom the word of God came, and the scripture cannot be broken; Say ye of him, whom the Father hath sanctified, and sent into the world, Thou blasphemest; because I said, I am the Son of God?"
John 10: 32-36 KJV

Obviously, even in the minds of those who sought after a deliverer, the prevailing question must have been, who could this person be, and where would he come from?

Undoubtedly he would have to be a Jew, because the Jews could never trust so great a task to anyone who was not of Jewish lineage. Matthew in the New Testament begins by tracing Jesus' bloodline forward through forty-two generations. However, this in and of itself would not be enough. The next daunting question would be, how could one mount this kind of a campaign without the support of the current religious leaders and their following? Or, how could you build such a following when the Roman leaders were so quick to respond to that kind of activity? In fact, a group calling itself the Zealots during that time became primary marks of aggression, for trying to militarily oppose the Roman domination of Palestine, and to incite a people's revolt against Roman tyranny and oppression. Because of the differences that existed between the religious sects of that day, i.e., Pharisees and Sadducees, there was little hope of any unified support from those who presided over the Temple and the synagogues. Also, the multi-cultural demographics of the area posed another challenge. There were Jews, Greeks, Romans and many other ethnic groups living in the region. What would be the single thread that would unite them, and turn their hearts toward God and this love He so urgently wanted them to receive?

"And leaving Nazareth, he came and dwelt in Capernaum, which is upon the sea coast, in the borders of Zabulon and Nephthalim: That it might be fulfilled which was spoken by Esaias the prophet, saying, The land of Zabulon, and the land of Nephthalim, by the way of the sea, beyond Jordan, Galilee of the Gentiles; The people which sat in darkness saw great light; and to them which sat in the region and shadow of death light is sprung up."

Matthew 4:13-16 KJV

Chapter 10

Blood Is Thicker Than Water

"For the LORD will pass through to smite the Egyptians; and when he seeth the blood upon the lintel, and on the two side posts, the LORD will pass over the door, and will not suffer the destroyer to come in unto your houses to smite you. And ye shall observe this thing for an ordinance to thee and to thy sons for ever."

Exodus 12:23-24 KJV

"And as they were eating, Jesus took bread, and blessed it, and brake it, and gave it to the disciples, and said, Take, eat; this is my body. And he took the cup, and gave thanks, and gave it to them, saying, Drink ye all of it; For this is my blood of the new testament, which is shed for many for the remission of sins."

Matthew 26:26-28 KJV

Now if there is one undisputable fact of human existence, it is that no matter what one's ethnic persuasion, gender or age might be, from the very beginning blood has been the single common link that ties all of mankind together. God has placed a significant amount of entitlement in the blood, even more so with those who remain under His blood covenant. From Genesis to Jesus even unto this very day, the blood represents a crimson rope that intertwines the Judeo-Christian Church into a perpetual oneness. Although the natural man may fade away and return to the dust, because of something as simple as the blood of a Passover lamb in Egypt, and the tremendous act of love that was carried out on Calvary, these blood ties will remain forever.

On the surface one would think that just having God's word of assurance would be enough for those who trust Him. But God also pre-ordained that the solution to the believers' dejection would not just be in a promise alone, but in the actual spilling of life giving blood.

When we look at the scripture in the Book of Exodus (*Exodus 12:23-24*), Israel was under inescapable bondage, being held fast by an adversary who at a glance appeared invincible in every sense of the word. For over 400 years the Egyptians loomed over Israel like a dark cloud, and through Pharaoh, a force of evil was raging. Little did the people of Egypt know that God was going to turn a whole nation from being victims of an Egyptian dynasty, into heirs of a victorious legacy. He would change the course of history, Jewish history, through something as simple as the blood of a lamb.

Now I want you to take note that when the angel of death was given his orders, he was not told to take inventory on anyone's life. This apparently was something that God was going to do later. And though all were not in place as far as their faith in God was concerned, because of who they were *His Chosen*, they remained covered by the blood. For those who insist on being judgmental against Israel, let us not forget that God always knew what He was doing. He knew that there would be many who were steeped in unbelief as a result of their suffering; but because blood is thicker than water, they didn't have to be perfect to be blessed. For a long while Israel's life was in the hands of a pharaoh, however there is nothing like God showing up in the middle of a crisis, to bring about a change in the hearts of those who might doubt. For years Israel's fate was in the hands of a man, but because of the blood it would be re-covered by a promise.

"For when God made promise to Abraham, because he could swear by no greater, he sware by himself, Saying, Surely blessing I will bless thee, and multiplying I will multiply thee."
Hebrews 6:13-14 KJV

If the blood of a lamb could deliver a nation under a prior Abrahamic Covenant, then certainly it is no small miracle that our lives are spared under this New Covenant, one also consummated by blood.

"For this is my blood of the new testament, which is shed for many for the remission of sins."
Matthew 26:28 KJV

It is a foregone conclusion that every sin you or I have been indicted for, accused and found guilty of was already contemplated by Jehovah Elohim Jehovah, (*I Am That I Am*). Jehovah Elohim Jehovah already knew the kinds of things that we could get into with the help of those forces that surround us. Not only has God seen us, but He had already preordained a place and time for our deliverance, and also the instrument He would use to bring us out. This is where the impossible becomes possible by Grace. For all whose hearts are opened towards Him, the time is always right now, the place is where you are, and the instrument is still an old rugged cross; so that we too, like the Hebrews in Egypt might be set free. Additionally, through God's Spirit we are able to gain deeper insight into the old family cliché that advances the notion, *blood is thicker than water*. By the shedding of Christ's blood, God has called us to a higher plane. Plane is defined as a surface that wholly contains every straight line joining any two points lying in it, the two points being Israel and the Church.

"Having predestinated us unto the adoption of children by Jesus Christ to himself, according to the good pleasure of his will, To the praise of the glory of his grace, wherein he hath made us accepted in the beloved."
Ephesians 1:5-6 KJV

God himself has engrafted us into the Beloved, and made us Mishpachah – family. This joining demands a higher or greater degree of adherence than most are willing to acknowledge. Our Father who is in Heaven is indeed speaking to His people in more positive ways. The Great Commission is not over. I know that some of us are already blessed exceedingly and abundantly, but that is no reason to sit down on God. Nowhere in the scriptures are we encouraged to seek out a comfortable spot, where we can sit and wait for the rapture. Instead we are told to be reaching, preaching, and teaching people that God is calling and empowering us to continue in our quest to set before Him a reconciled Church.

"Being confident of this very thing, that he which hath begun a good work in you will perform it until the day of Jesus Christ:"

Philippians 1:6 KJV

This is why I have a problem defining a Conservative Christian. In every society or organized group of people two types are always recognized, the conservative looking back to the past and the progressive looking forward to the future. I have yet to understand how Conservatism and Christianity can be co-laborers. God is always calling us out of our comfort zones, showing up when we least expect Him and asking us to do things our uncommitted lazy side does not normally want to do.

God is moving His Church to a new era – not one where we just sit content in an assembly, but instead one where the Church is so fired up they can't wait to get in the presence of their next target. God wants us to understand that this thing is a whole lot bigger than we are. He wants all of us to know that our very being goes a lot further than the person we see in the mirror every morning. His plan for us is more than that which meets the natural eye.

Why is blood thicker than water; its by the reminiscence of oneness that the blood corroborates. God will continue to shape mold and position His new covenant, raising us together Jew and Gentile, as He prepares to present us to the entire world as *one new man.*

"For he is our peace, who hath made both one, and hath broken down the middle wall of partition between us; Having abolished in his flesh the enmity, even the law of commandments contained in ordinances; for to make in himself of twain one new man, so making peace;"

Ephesians 2:14-15 KJV

It is God who determined that the predominate solution to Israel's co-existence, co-laboring, co-destiny with the Christian Church would be found in *THE BLOOD.*

"Wherein God, willing more abundantly to shew unto the heirs of promise the immutability of his counsel, confirmed it by an oath: That by two immutable things, in which it was impossible for God to lie, we might have a strong consolation, who have fled for refuge to lay hold upon the hope set before us:"

Hebrews 6:17-18 KJV

Chapter 11

The Intrusion of the Strong Man

"No man can enter into a strong man's house, and spoil his goods, except he will first bind the strong man; and then he will spoil his house.'

Mark 3:27 KJV

As you may know, the strong man Jesus is referring to is Satan the adversary. An outsider who had managed through violent assault to enter into, lay siege upon and take possession of another's house or property. In order for the rightful owner to recover their goods, they must first uncover a way to bind that strong man. Of course, the only way to do that is to enlist the services or employ the actions of a stronger man. Hence, the Jerusalem Council augmented by the true Church.

"For the eyes of the Lord run to and fro throughout the whole earth, to show himself strong in the behalf of them whose heart is perfect toward him. Herein thou hast done foolishly: therefore from henceforth thou shalt have wars."

2 Chronicles 16:9 KJV

"And ye shall seek me, and find me, when ye shall search for me with all your heart."

Jeremiah 29:13 KJV

What both these writers, Solomon the King and Jeremiah the Prophet are advocating, is that one sincere heartfelt outpouring to God, can be more successful at binding the strong man, than an entire army fully arrayed for battle. It seems that the Israelites like so many other chosen of God, had never experienced any length of time when they did not have to deal with the advances of the strong man and his agents, each seeing himself as a strong man. All of these antagonists were determined to deny the well being of God's chosen vessels.

"Thus saith the LORD of hosts; Behold, I will save my people from the east country, and from the west country; And I will

bring them, and they shall dwell in the midst of Jerusalem: and they shall be my people, and I will be their God, in truth and in righteousness."

Zechariah 8:7-8 KJV

There was a span of two hundred years between the conquering of Babylon by Cyrus the Great of Persia, a strong man: the re-founding of the Jewish nation under the leadership of Nehemiah and Ezra, and the destruction of the Persian Empire by Alexander the Great, another strong man. Alexander was a young Greek general who defeated the Persian Emperor Darius III at a place called Issus. Physically speaking all these men and the armies which they commanded were huge and very strong. The great Empire created by Alexander to date has never been rivaled. It has been noted that his army of Macedonian and Greek troops numbered close to thirty thousand foot soldiers and five thousand Calvary. All of these well trained, well equipped, strongmen were able to overthrow the highly fragmented and unorganized Persian Empire within a four year period. Alexander's campaign surged without any credible resistance. It spanned from Asia Minor to Egypt, from Egypt to Central Asia, and then to the Indus Valley in India. Wherever he went Alexander founded or re-founded Greek style cities with his own name, spreading Hellenistic (Greek) city-based culture over the whole empire. By 332 B.C.E., Alexander the strong man conquered Judea. As a result, the influence of Hellenism on the Jews increased. The strong arm of the strong man was in place, acting as a vice to hold and secure the furtherance of the Greek culture into the lives, and subsistence of the Jewish people. In fact it soon became necessary if one wanted to be successful, to obtain a Greek education. Many Jews accepted this intrusion of the strong man readily.

They often welcomed those Jews who spoke Greek and had adopted Greek culture to the temple when they returned from pilgrimage. For the conservative Jews however, this whole Hellenistic (Greek) idea was not a good one. They hated the Greek customs and influences on their people. Activities such as wrestling and athletics were highly detested. This was mainly because they were all in some way connected to Greek mythology. The clear challenge facing the Jewish Nation at that time was how a psychologically conquered people, could combat the aggressions and intrusions of the strong man. I say psychologically conquered because even to this very day, Israel's enemies still fear their God. The question to be answered by Israel's enemies then and now is how do we keep this remnant from calling on their God with one voice?

"Submit yourselves therefore to God. Resist the devil, and he will flee from you."

James 4:7 KJV

This Scripture was written by the Apostle James, the last man standing in behalf of the original Jerusalem Council. The operative words here are submit and resist. Here is how the Apostle Paul addresses this same question of how to rebound, from the intrusion of the strong man.

"Finally, my brethren, be strong in the Lord, and in the power of his might."

Ephesians 6:10 KJV

Both the Apostles James and Paul are talking about a surrender of a different sort, not into the hands of the strong man, but rather a yielding or a relinquishing of our plans and programs over to the plan that God has prearranged. To publicly express a willingness to take part in the promotion of His predetermined, providential plan.

As a result of Israel's desperate need for revival at that time, a variety of religious groups emerged within Judaism. Two of these groups were the Pharisees and Sadducees. Although they differed on their approach in some areas to the Jewish religion, they both held a disdain for the Greek or Hellenistic mythologies and ideals. The Pharisees insisted on the strict observance of Jewish ritual laws. They demanded that those of their groups obey rules of food and purity. They also isolated themselves from non-Pharisees. These men were very influential in the Jews Supreme Court and legislative body, the Sanhedrin.

The Sadducees on the other hand had exercised considerable political and spiritual influence. Most of them were wealthy, and included among their group was the High Priest and President of the Sanhedrin. Both groups understood however, the need for resistance. They were well aware of the fact that religious tolerance should not be confused with religious freedom. Here is a present day example; when lobbyist for instance, can influence the government to bring pressure on the Church to accept ordinances and practices of those who stand in opposition to its beliefs, then that state of affairs must be recognized for what it is, religious tolerance. In other words you are allowed to have Church, but certainly not religious freedom.

After the death of Alexander the Great in 323 B.C., a Greek General by the name of Antiochus, another strong man, launched an attack on the Jewish religion in 170 B.C. He longed for the wealth of the Temple in Jerusalem. Antiochus sent in troops to put down unrest and resistance. These troops looted the city and pulled down its walls, but they didn't destroy the Temple. However, by 70 A.D., Titus the son of the Roman Emperor Vespasian, another strongman laid siege to Jerusalem with an army of four legions. Having breached the walls, Roman troops stormed the Temple; and by September of that year the Temple with all of its splendor and treasure was looted and destroyed.

"And as some spake of the temple, how it was adorned with goodly stones and gifts, he said, As for these things which ye behold, the days will come, in the which there shall not be left one stone upon another, that shall not be thrown down."

Luke 21:5-6

One can only imagine how often these undervalued, disregarded people had to remind themselves, and those of their bloodlines, that no word from God would ever fail. One strong man after another seemed bent on robbing the Jews of their destiny as sole heirs of this undersized piece of real estate which caps the African Continent. In assessing the extraordinary value that the world powers have assigned to its strategic location, I submit that she, Israel should be recognized as the Crown of Africa. What an encouraging thought considering the current state of Africa today. Unfortunately, all of the strongmen in Israel's life have not gone away. I challenge the Church to open its eyes and be bold enough to identify the next strong man. He will be the one standing between Israel and her Divine Destiny as the center of the Christian Church.

Chapter 12

Quitting Is Not an Option

"For we have not followed cunningly devised fables, when we made known unto you the power and coming of our Lord Jesus Christ, but were eyewitnesses of his majesty."
2 Peter 1:16 KJV

Early Christianity is closer to Judaism than the devotees of either religion have usually wished to admit. Both Christian Theologians and Orthodox Jews have underestimated the Judo-Christian bond. It was only gradually that Christianity severed its connection with the Jewish community and became transformed into a gentile religion. The story of Israel has immense historic significance for all Christians. Besides Jesus himself, Judaism gave Christians the one, the Living God. It contributed a sacred book, its own testament and thereby paved the way for the New Testament. It passed on a historic tradition that made life purposeful and history full of meaning. The Gospels are a record of Jewish life in Judea and in Galilee, during the early decades of the first century.

The early Christians when they set out to convert the Gentiles took the Old Testament as their text which gave them an unequal advantage over their rivals. No other religion in the empire possessed a book charged with such vitality and eloquence. Israel had given to Christianity the prophets of truth and righteousness as well as the belief in the Messiah. This is exactly what the Apostle Peter was referring to in our opening passage when he stated, "but (we) were eyewitnesses to His majesty." All of the Disciples of Christ had very unique experiences during their conversions. However, nowhere in Christian history is there evidence of a single conversion to Christ, which would have a worldwide impact as that of Saul of Tarsus, later called Paul the Apostle. Saul was a leading participant in the persecution that began with the slaying of Stephen.

"And in those days, when the number of the disciples was multiplied, there arose a murmuring of the Grecians against the Hebrews, because their widows were neglected in the daily ministration. Then the twelve called the multitude of the disciples unto them, and said, It is not reason that we should leave the word of God, and serve tables. Wherefore, brethren, look ye out among you seven men of honest report, full of the Holy Ghost and wisdom, whom we may appoint over this business. But we will give ourselves continually to prayer, and to the ministry of the word. And the saying pleased the whole multitude: and they chose Stephen, a man full of faith and of the Holy Ghost, and Philip, and Prochorus, and Nicanor, and Timon, and Parmenas, and Nicolas a proselyte of Antioch:"

Acts 6:1-5 KJV

"And Stephen, full of faith and power, did great wonders and miracles among the people."

Acts 6:8 KJV

"And Saul was consenting unto his death. And at that time there was a great persecution against the Church which was at Jerusalem; and they were all scattered abroad throughout the regions of Judaea and Samaria, except the apostles. And devout men carried Stephen to his burial, and made great lamentation over him. As for Saul, he made havoc of the Church, entering into every house, and haling men and women committed them to prison."

Acts 8:1-3 KJV

After the stoning of this faithful Disciple, the Church at Jerusalem was scattered widely except the Apostles. The Jerusalem Council remained, they were steadfast. Some of the members escaped to Damascus and others fled 300 miles to Antioch, the capital of Syria of which the great province of Palestine was a part. At Antioch these few Judeans went into the Jewish synagogue and there gave their testimony for Jesus as the Messiah.

In every synagogue a place was set apart for Gentile worship-pers. Many of these heard the gospel at Antioch and embraced the faith of Christ.

"Then tidings of these things came unto the ears of the Church which was in Jerusalem: and they sent forth Barnabas, that he should go as far as Antioch. Then departed Barnabas to Tarsus, for to seek Saul: And when he had found him, he brought him unto Antioch. And it came to pass, that a whole year they as-sembled themselves with the Church, and taught much people. And the disciples were called Christians first in Antioch. And in these days came prophets from Jerusalem unto Antioch."
Acts 11:22, 25-27 KJV

As a result of this powerful spirit of love and devotion a Church grew up wherein Jews and Gentiles worshipped to-gether as equals in privilege. It has been noted; when people share common needs, struggles and enemies it can have a gal-vanizing effect. What a staunch testimonial to Judeo-Christian history. One can only imagine what this absorbing God inspired relationship would look like, had it not been for the devastat-ing onslaught that was orchestrated by those whose hatred for Israel ran so deep, that it would be perpetuated for centuries, even to this very day.

"We are troubled on every side, yet not distressed; we are per-plexed, but not in despair; persecuted, but not forsaken; cast down, but not destroyed."
2 Corinthians 4:8-9 KJV

Consider the first Church almost still-born, every thing was going wrong that could go wrong. These were some perplexing bewildering times for the Disciples who were a rare breed in-deed. As the pains of abandonment ran rapid again, they found their faith being challenged in ways that many Christians of our day could hardly imagine. Yet, they refused to back down and they refused to quit. Based on a decision rendered by the Jerusalem Council, the Church was given permission to expand its missionary efforts to include people of all races and of every land.

With the blessings of the Council, the Church continued to grow until its area of recruitment included the entire Roman Empire... from the Atlantic coast of Spain in the west, to the Black Sea in the east, from the Rhine in the north to the Nile in the south. The relentless campaign of the Christian Church was made even easier, because the Romans had connected these large swatches of land, by building a highly developed network of well constructed roads. But as the Church made its trek throughout the Roman Provinces, so did the evil adversary pursuing her.

"Be sober, be vigilant; because your adversary the devil, as a roaring lion, walketh about, seeking whom he may devour: Whom resist stedfast in the faith knowing that the same afflictions are accomplished in your brethren that are in the world."
1 Peter 5:8-9 KJV

So the Church was forced to build her legacy on a trail of blood, sweat and tears. For many who opposed the Church it was just a matter of economics and social acceptance. Heathenism was hospitable to new forms and objects of worship. When the people of a province or city desired to promote trade or immigration, they would build temples to the deities worshipped in other lands in order that their citizens would have a place of worship. Christianity however, presented a problem to this kind of religious inclusion because it opposed all worship except to its own God. The Christians were therefore regarded as unsocial and gloom; as Atheist having no gods and haters of their fellow men. Even when it came down to showing their loyalty to the reigning emperor, by offering incense to images of him that were set up in certain places, as one would to a god. They were steadfast in their beliefs and were determined to remain loyal to the doctrine that they had embraced. There would be no incense offered to the emperor or any other deity, no, not even a pinch.

As time went on the leaders of the Church were taken down in order to break its spirit and weaken its morale. The first of these was James, the brother of Jesus. James was a loyal supporter of Jewish customs and practices and a recognized leader among Jewish Christians. He was slain in the Temple around 62 A.D. In the year 64 A.D. a large part of Rome was destroyed by a great fire. It had been reported that the fire had been started by Nero the worst of all the Roman Emperors. In order to clear himself, Nero blamed the Christians for the devastation. This promptly gave rise to a terrible persecution; thousands were tortured and put to death. Nero had declared an all out war on the Christian Nation. Multitudes of Christians were burned as "living torches" while the Emperor drove his chariot among them nude and playing a fiddle. In Rome, the capital of the most powerful Empire of the western world, in 67 A.D. the Apostle Peter, a man who was recognized by Paul as one of the pillars of the Church, was crucified upside down. In 68 A.D. Peter's death was followed by the beheading of Paul in Rome. Some called it poetic justice and others called it a twist of faith. To this observer it seemed ironic that the gardens of Nero, the courts where the Apostle Paul and the Apostle Peter were both slain or martyred, the place where countless thousands of Christians were slaughtered like animals, are now the seat of the Vatican palace; the home of the Roman Catholic Pontiff and recognized by millions as the center of the Christian world. Just as the believers who blazed the trail before us refused to dishonor the directives of God, and the patterns set by Jesus himself, including the formation of a Christian Council in Jerusalem; neither should we dishonor or ignore this mandate that God has set before us.

When I wrote this chapter, I found myself being haunted by the words of an old hymn:

> Let us go back, let us go back;
> back to our father's praying
> ground.
>
> God is not pleased, God is
> not pleased; Let us go back
> on bended knees.
>
> Too far away we have strayed,
> Just now and then a soul is
> saved.
>
> Let us go back, back to our
> father's praying ground.

I submit to you that the "praying ground" could be no other place than Jerusalem in Israel.

Chapter 13

The Calm before a Storm

"See that ye refuse not him that speaketh. For if they escaped not who refused him that spake on earth, much more shall not we escape, if we turn away from him that speaketh from heaven: whose voice then shook the earth: but now he hath promised, saying, yet once more I shake not the earth only, but also heaven."

Hebrews 12:25-26 KJV

God is adamant over the fact that for this generation there will be a fundamental shaking that will be difficult if not impossible to ignore. "See that you refuse not him that is speaking." Since the tragedy of 911 in Manhattan, all across the Middle East, Russia, China and Europe the world has been holding it's breath in the wake of one explosive event after another. From one side of the globe to the other, nature has been shaking the very foundation of our planet with hurricanes, tsunamis, earthquakes, firestorms and melting ice. Every day more of our wildlife, rain forest and ice caps are starting to disappear. The health of our global economy has all but collapsed. Billions of dollars, euros and pounds are being lost at an alarming rate and great corporations are falling, taking with them the savings of millions of people. That is why we can no longer afford a form of godliness that has no power.

As long as the Church was Jewish in membership and even afterward while it was being managed by practical men of the Jewish type, such as the Apostles Peter and Paul, there was not a lot of room for imaginary and speculative thinking. But when the Church found its largest constituency among the Greeks and especially the mystical unbalance Greeks of Asia Minor, all sorts of strange opinions and theories arose and grew to power.

When it was determined by the Jerusalem Council that a Gentile did not have to convert to Judaism to become a follower of Christ, this opened the door to widespread Church growth

100

among the Gentiles. So many Gentiles were saved that the Jewish believer became a minority. However, history shows that as the center of the Christian faith moved from "Jerusalem to Rome" it became increasingly Hellenized, adopting pagan customs and philosophies rather than the God ordained practices and beliefs of the Bible. At the same time Christianity became increasingly anti-Jewish. By 135 A.D. the Romans renamed Israel "Syria-Palestine".

The New Testament uses the land of Israel twice (Matthews 2:20-21) but never uses the name Palestine or Palestinian. By 306 A.D. Constantine, a Roman Emperor came into power. He was a master politician. He tried to attract heathens to Christianity by modifying pagan customs and festivals and giving them Christian meanings. This would still allow Christians to keep their traditions. The group he did not like was the Jews since they had rebelled against Rome. The Church was more than willing to follow Constantine's lead in order to avoid persecution. Constantine built many Churches and monasteries, but the Jews were not permitted in Jerusalem except for one day a year. On this day they were allowed to mourn the destruction of the Temple.

Centuries later the Emperor Constantine would express the anti-Judaic sentiments of the bishops of the Church world when he wrote, "Let us therefore have nothing in common with this odious people the Jews, for we have received from our savior a different way. Strive and pray continually that the purity of your souls may not be sullied by fellowship with the customs of these most wicked men . . . all should unite in desiring that which sound reason appears to demand in avoiding all participation in the perjured conduct of the Jews. Prior to Constantine's rhetoric, "for we have received from our savior a different way," the Apostle Paul wrote:

"But though we, or an angel from heaven, preach any other gospel unto you than that which we have preached unto you, let him be accursed. As we said before, so say I now again, if any man preach any other gospel unto you, than that ye have received, let him be accursed.
Galatians 1:8-9 KJV

Without fervent Jewish participation there would be no Christian Church. That is why we must have a Jewish-Christian Council in Jerusalem. In the Gospel of John Chapter 7, Jesus celebrates the Feast of Tabernacles; in that same Gospel of John Chapter 10, Jesus is in the Temple for Hanukkah or Passover, it is the feast in which Jesus was killed for the redemption of all men. We are told to celebrate "the Feast" in 1 Corinthians 5:8. The Feast of Early Fruits is the Feast in which Jesus was raised from the dead. Pentecost, the latter first fruits is the Feast in which The Holy Spirit was sent to baptize the believers. People in Jerusalem during Shavot (Shavuot) or Pentecost were amazed that the 120 who were all Galileans, were talking about God in different languages (Acts 2:7).

Peter and Andrew are the first two Jewish fishermen to follow Jesus, they lived in Galilee. The next two followers of Jesus were James and John also fishermen from Galilee. Phillip, Bartholomew, Thomas, Matthew, Samuel, Thaddeus, Simon and Judas were all Jewish.

In the Book of Matthew we can see where Jesus' plan was to first establish the base of the Christian Church in Jerusalem. He gives these twelve Jewish men the following instructions; *". . . go not into the way of the Gentiles, and into any city of the Samaritans enter ye not: But go rather to the lost sheep of the house of Israel."*
Matt 10:5-6 KJV

"And the word of God increased; and the number of the disciples multiplied in Jerusalem greatly; and a great company of the priests were obedient to the faith."
Acts 6:7 KJV

Acts 15 highlights the Council members who met in Jerusalem to figure out how to include the Gentiles in the Church. By verse 22, a letter had been drafted to the Gentile believers about requirements of following Jesus. In Acts 21, Paul arrives in Jerusalem to see James and the Elders of the Church. Paul reveals to them what God had done among the Gentiles and this was their response, "You see brother, how many thousands of Jews have believed and all of them are zealous for the law." We must alert a sleeping Church to the fact that it was no coincidence that when the Jewish biblical heritage of the Church was replaced with paganism, intimacy with God was watered down. The supernatural power of God was replaced with the politics and traditions of men. When the Church walked away from its biblical Jewish roots it abandoned God's pattern. The original Church split was the division between Jew and Gentile.

"Love worketh no ill to his neighbor: therefore, love is the fulfilling of the law. And that, knowing the time, that now it is high time to awake out of sleep: for now is our salvation nearer than when we believed."
Romans 13:10-11 KJV

We should let the wisdom of this statement from the Apostle Paul serve as a warning to us, to use caution as we approach the non-Christian Jews; those who insist on protecting the traditions and beliefs passed down through generations. Be mindful that the strength of their argument can be extracted from the character, attitude and history of the Christian Church. This was a Church that began with Jews and Gentiles walking hand in hand, promoting an idea that they collectively had embraced and exercised. Later the same Church that many Jews gave rise, credence and their lives to, would be turned into a deadly sword against them.

With the fire of anti-Semitism pouring out of his mouth, the Roman Emperor Constantine retained some of the heathen titles of the Emperor as that of "Pontifex Maximus", which means Chief Priest, both the head of the Empire and the head of the Church as well; a title by the way, held by all of the Popes since. Because of his strategies and political savvy, the city of Rome was replaced by Constantinople, which is now Istanbul, as the capital of the world. During that same period however, the Roman Church was growing in prestige and power and the Bishop of Rome now entitled Pope, was claiming the throne of authority over the entire Christian world. Everywhere Bishops controlled the Churches, but the question that was constantly arising was who should control the Bishops? What Bishop would take the place of the Emperor over the Church?

The presiding Bishops in certain cities soon came to be called "Metropolitans" and afterwards "Patriarchs." There were patriarchs at Jerusalem, Antioch, Alexander, Constantinople and Rome. The Roman Bishop took the title of "Papa", "Father" later changed to Pope. Between these five Patriarchs were frequent contests; but the question finally narrowed down to the choice between the Patriarch of Constantinople and the Pope of Rome as head of the Church. In the end Rome presented the greatest argument. Rome was the only Church which named as its founders two Apostles, Peter and Paul, both Jews. The contention was that Peter was the first Bishop of Rome and so he must have been "Papa", "Father" or Pope. But Peter was present when Jesus spoke these words in the book of Matthew.

"And call no man your father upon the earth: for one is your Father, which is in heaven".

Matthew 23:9 KJV

Although the Apostle Peter did spend time with the Church in Rome, we know that his ending was a lot less glamorous than that of a Pope.

Within 25 years after Constantine's death, the Roman Empire became saturated with moral and political decay. In less than 140 years the Western Roman Empire, which had endured a thousand years, was swept out of existence by hoards of barbarians who came from everywhere. However, the Christianity of that decadent age was still vital and aggressive, and converted many of these conquering races. In turn their vigorous blood contributed to make a new European race. Ultimately, the decline and fall of the imperial power at Rome only increased the influence throughout Europe of the Roman Church and the Popes.

The beginning of the 7th century found Jews inhabiting most areas in Europe. I believe here that a distinction should be made between two terms: exile, which means a compulsory banishment, and Diaspora which signifies a voluntary scattering. Both have been part of Jewish existence from their earliest history. Exile became Diaspora when the Jews adjusted themselves to their new environment. The Jews had first arrived in Europe in the wake of the conquering Roman legions, but now it had become increasingly difficult for the Jews to navigate successfully through the turbulent wars of the newly converted and newly fanatic European nations. Once again what the Jews of Europe would learn was consistent with their past, and what would turn out to be consistent with much of their future. Just when they began to feel at home anywhere else but Israel, what they would be experiencing would be nothing more than the calm before a storm.

As relationships with the Christians deteriorated, the Jews of Spain in a last ditch effort to prove their innocence, tried to show that their ancestors had left Palestine long before the time of Christ, and hence, had no part in his crucifixion. Needless to say arguments of this kind were of no avail. The oppressive measures reached a climax in 613 A.D. when the King of Spain demanded that all Jews accept baptism. It was the first time such a decree had affected an entire country. Hundreds caved into the pressure and converted. Yet despite these mass conversions and the severe punishments handed out to those who later "relapsed" into Judaism; whole communities managed to survive. Many Jews who had accepted baptism at the point of swords, reverted back to Judaism as soon as the imminent danger passed.

The high level of persecution that had to be endured in the 7th century led to the almost total devastation of Spanish Jewry. It is astonishing that so many Jews clung to their own values. Nothing less than an unshakable conviction of moral and religious faith could have enabled them to survive the relentless wave of terror and forced conversions - *Convert or Die*. During that same period in the Middle East the two chief towns of Arabia were Mecca and Medina. Mecca more than a trading center was also the site of the Kabba, a small temple of black stone, the cornerstone of which was a meteorite - and as such a center of religious pilgrimage.

Medina at that time was a smaller city founded it is said by Jews who had originally come there from Yemen. Until 525 A.D., the princes of Medina had for centuries professed Judaism as their religion. It was against this back drop that the Career of the Prophet Mohammed unfolded. Born in Mecca in 750 C.E. (Christian era) of poor humble stock, Mohammed rose from a mere camel driver to become first the leader of a caravan, and then the leader of the entire Arab people. It is said that Mohammed was intrigued by the religious beliefs of both Jews and Christians. Mohammed felt himself possessed of prophetic power, a power whose supernatural provision was confirmed by occasional visitations from heaven. He saw himself as uniting in his person two distinct functions, that of the Prophet, and that of the Apostle. His earlier followers were slaves and people of humble origin. The well to do shunned him and saw him as a threat to their way of life, and they began to aggressively confront him. In 622 C.E., fearing for his life, Mohammed fled with a few close followers to Medina. The date of this flight known in Arabic as the Bejira marks the beginning of the Moslem calendar.

In arriving at Medina he met with unexpected resistance from the Jews. Angered by their opposition and jealous of their financial success, Mohammed conceived a hatred for Jews. To propagate or spawn his new religion of Islam, Mohammed selected a novel method. Most of his converts were won on the field of battle where the beaten, usually members of trading caravans from Mecca, were given the alternative to convert or die. And still today "Death to Israel and all her infidel allies," is the battle cry that burns within the hearts of the Islamic extremists across the globe.

Just as in the beginning, Adam's son Cain slew his brother Abel in a jealous rage because of the apparent favor of God that was upon Abel's life; Islamic extremists are convinced that as long as the Jews exist, they will never receive their rightful place as rulers of the Middle East, and eventually the entire world. To this end, they will align themselves with anyone who shares their commitment to bring Israel to a place of total extinction. Ishmael the approved, against Isaac the appointed, to whom God has said:

"For I know the thoughts that I think toward you, saith the lord, thoughts of peace, and not of evil, to give you an expected end."

Jeremiah 29:11 KJV

Therefore the conclusion of the matter is that no counter effort can ever be successful against that which God has already ordained. Not even by a powerful, influential religious group such as radical Islam; although in their hearts and minds they have sworn to stop at nothing to reach their goal, which is the total destruction of Israel and her allies in the West.

This is the same kind of fervor and dedication that the Christian Church must have as she embarks on her campaign, not only to speak out against anti-Semitism world-wide, and to stand with Israel in all her endeavors, but also to recreate a Jewish-Christian Council in Jerusalem. God has made it emphatically clear that our greatest blessing lies before us, if Israel is not left to stand alone.

"And I will make of thee a great nation, and I will bless thee, and make thy name great, and thou shalt be a blessing: and I will bless them that bless thee, and curse him that curseth thee: and in thee shall all families of the earth be blessed."
Genesis 12:2 KJV

Herein rests a truth that can never be ignored. There are few nations and people in this world whose lives have not been impacted by a Jew or a group of Jews in one form or another. Some of the greatest inventions and innovations in the areas of science, medicine, agriculture, manufacturing, communications, teaching, music, dance and the arts in general, have come from the Jewish mind. Except we be guilty of treachery of the highest level and blatant hypocrisy, we can no more blame the Jews for the death of Christ and make them accountable, than we could blame every Southerner for the atrocities of the American slave trade, or every German for the Holocaust. It is true that some Jews were involved in this event, but we must keep in mind that it was an event ordained of God. Those involved were only mirroring the sentiments and rebellious attitudes of humankind even until this day.

Our Bible tells us that God so loved the world **"that He GAVE His only begotten Son."** If any blame must be assigned for the death of Jesus than it must be placed upon all of mankind. Those involved in the most controversial event of all time, only did what men have always done. If we don't like the message we destroy the messenger. Most of us have rebelled against the teachings of Christ, especially when it comes to recognizing the Jew and Jerusalem first. And so to lay the blame of our shortcomings, and rebellious attitudes squarely at the feet of the Jews is something that God will no longer allow. Anti-Semitism in or out of the Church must be challenged aggressively. If as Christians, we sincerely believe that Israel is God's gift to the nations, and that He is the architect of this movement, then we have no choice but to follow His biblical blueprint to preserve her integrity, strength and place in the world.

It is no secret that those who wish to end the marriage between Israel and the United States are busy making plans to do so. It is also no secret that what most of us are embracing as peace and safety, is nothing more than the calm before a storm. As their weapons increase whether they are human bodies or long range missiles, they are definitely becoming more and more efficient. If the events of 911 taught us anything, it is the certainty that we are all in the line of fire. Unlike anytime in its recent history, the Church must prepare for war, with faith in God as our ultimate weapon.

"The Lord is my strength and song, and he is become my salvation: he is my God, and I will prepare him an habitation; my father's God, and I will exalt him. The Lord is a man of war: the Lord is his name."

Exodus 15:2-3 KJV

Chapter 14

The Shadow of Death

"The Lord is my shepherd: I shall not want. He maketh me to lie down in green pastures: He leadeth me beside the still waters. He restoreth my soul: He leadeth me in the paths of righteousness for His name's sake. Yea, though I walk through the valley of the shadow of death, I will fear no evil for thou art with me; thy rod and thy staff they comfort me. Thou preparest a table before me in the presence of mine enemies: thou anointest my head with oil; my cup runneth over. Surely goodness and mercy shall follow me all the day s of my life: and I will dwell in the house of the Lord for ever.

Psalms 23:1-6 KJV

For centuries this Psalm has held its unrivaled position as one of the premier writings of all religious literature in the world. No matter what age, race or circumstance one might find themselves identified with; there is something about this Psalm that is able to bring an inner peace and quiet comfort to the soul. It has been read by and spoken into the ear of many disheartened and frightened seekers of absolution. It is indeed in a class all of its own; as it breathes confidence and trust that we are not being asked to take this journey all alone.

"Yea though I walk through the valley of the shadow of death, I will fear no evil for thou art with me." There is a people who have walked through this valley and under the shadow of death for an untold number of years. One reason or another has been assigned to the Jews as justification for their annihilation. Throughout their history, these people have been accused of being land grabbers, leeches and even murderers of Jesus. Yet somewhere deep within their collective being, there remains this acute awareness that they were never alone. God Himself formed these people, sent them through the loins of Abraham and promised them multiple blessings. These are the people that would forever be called Chosen and used as a signal to the world that Israel's God was God.

A drawn out people, that He would use to be a conduit through which to send the redeemer of the world. They had not earned or asked for this, but because of the sovereignty and grace of God, He tagged them and in numerous ways announced that they would be His people.

When they went down into the land of Egypt there were seventy, when they received their freedom they were a mixed multitude of possibly more than a million. They would then go into the land of Canaan and conquer that land under God's power and authority. This was a strange people that God had created for Himself; a people whom He would fight for and slay kings for. He would literally open and part rivers and seas and bring down walls for this, His people. Again and again, God would establish them in places where they would enjoy vineyards that they didn't plant, live in homes they did not build, and truly be blessed above measure. So much so, that those who were considered giants, and all who had previously occupied the lands (the Philistines, Canaanites, Hittites), and many others had to move because God had sanctioned His people with His blessings. As they went to and fro He could always find a witness in every generation. When a generation rose up and did that which seemed right in their own eyes, God Himself would teach, mold and shape them, and prepare them through human experiences. Judgment is a hard teacher, but nevertheless it does teach.

Therefore, when these people who were set apart for a divine mission found themselves under the tyranny and leadership of their enemies, they cried out to God and He heard them. We must as one voice and one people, speak out loud on Israel's behalf, because we all know that she has more than her share of those who will speak out loud against her.

In 1543, Martin Luther set out his "Honest advice as to how Jews should be treated." First he wrote, "their synagogues should be set on fire, and whatever does not burn up should be covered or spread over with dirt so that no one may be able to see a cinder or stone of it." Secondly, "Jewish homes should likewise be broken down or destroyed." Third, "Jews should be put under one roof, or in a stable like gypsies, in order that they may realize that they are not masters of our land." Fourth, "they should be put to work, to earn their living by the sweat of their noses, or if regarded to be too dangerous, these poisonous bitter worms should be stripped of their belongings which they have earned or extorted usuriously from us, and driven out of the country for all times."

Luther's advice was typical of the anti-Semitic venom of its time; mass expulsion was commonplace in medieval policy. Jews were driven out of almost every European country including England, France, Spain, Portugal and Bohemia. In Italy, Jews were to be confined to a special part of the towns called "the ghetto," which would be the same term used to describe certain residential areas housing Black Americans all over the United States. For the Jews, reoccurring expulsions and the oppression that fueled them continued until the 19th century. Not a decade passed without Jews in one European state or another, being accused of murdering Christian children in order to use their blood in the baking of Passover bread. This "blood libel", which prompted increased violence against Jews coupled with a two thousand year old history of Jew hatred, reflected deep prejudices which no amount of modern or liberal education seemed able to overcome.

In the war which came to Europe in August 1914, Jews served in every army and on opposite sides of the trenches and the wire. German Jews fought and died as German patriarchs, shooting at British Jews who fought and died as British patriarchs. Jews and non-Jews alike fought as Germans for duty and the father land. When the war ended in 1918 Jewish soldiers, sailors and airmen had filled the roles of honor, the field hospitals and the military cemeteries. After 1918, Jews found themselves under new flags and new national allegiances. But by 1919 in Berlin Germany, the nation's capital, there were clashes between Jews and anti-Semites. On August 14, 1919, the Berlin correspondent of The Times reported, "indications of growing anti-Semitism are becoming more frequent." A blatant display of this anti-Semitism was shown by one of Germany's new political groups, the **Nazi**onal Socialist German Worker's Party, soon to be better known as the Nazi party after the first two syllables of **Nazi**onal. With only sixty members, they set forth a program for the return of Germany's colonies which had been lost at the time of Germany's defeat. Of their 25 point program, point four was the most racialist one. "None but members of the nation may be citizens of the State. None but those of German blood, whatever their creed, may be members of the **Nazi**on. No Jew therefore, may be a member of the nation." Another point demanded that all Jews who had come to Germany since 1914 should be forced to leave. The anti-Jewish sections of the Nazi party's program had been drafted by three members, one of them being Adolf Hitler - another strongman.

On August 13, 1920, Hitler spoke for two hours in a Munich beer cellar on the theme "Why we are against the Jew." During his speech he promised his listeners that "his party and his party alone will free you from the power of the Jew." Hitler introduced a new slogan, *"anti-Semites of the world unite."* A year later Hitler formed a group within his own party known as the SA, its members were storm troopers. Throughout Berlin the group wasted no time going to work. Many Jews were beaten it was reported "until the blood streamed down their heads and faces, and their backs and shoulders were bruised, many fainted and were left lying in the streets."

By 1933 the German government gave legal status to non-Jewish Germans as "Aryan." Hitler had formerly divided German citizens into two groups all across Germany. German cities competed in zealous pursuit of the new Aryan idea. One could either be a German or one could be a Jew. The first Jews had reached German soil in Roman times. Jews had lived in Germany for a thousand years. Their contributions to the German society were many but now it was all over. All over Germany, Jews were singled out for violent assault. Many left Germany as exiles. More than five thousand immigrated to Palestine. By the end of 1933 more than 26,000 German Jews had been taken into "protective custody." These concentration camps or Gestapo prisons would ultimately become nothing more than death traps, where a total of six million men, women and children were caged, gassed and murdered like animals, and then buried in mass graves.

The last week of October 1933, in reaction to the growth of Jewish immigrants to Palestine, Arab rioters attacked public buildings in Nablus, Jaffa and Jerusalem. The British drove back rioters leaving 26 Arabs dead. Nazi propaganda broadcasts beamed to Palestine. Syria and Egypt helped ensure that Arab hostility towards the Jewish immigrants would be kept as high as possible. Hitler's monster plan for the Jews became clear in November, 1938 the "night of broken glass." During the night, as well as breaking into tens of thousands of shops and homes, the storm troopers set fire to 191 synagogues. And if it was thought the fire might endanger nearby buildings, they smashed the synagogues as much as possible with hammers and axes. Hitler's anti-Semitism was raging and to most observers the Jews of Europe were doomed. In a conquest of continental Europe in March 1938, Hitler absorbed Austria into the German ranks. In September he invaded Czechoslovakia and later Poland which had been home to over three million Jews. Britain and France declared war two weeks later and the Soviet army occupied half of Poland, but by the end of the month, in short order, Poland was a bleeding corpse devastated by what was called the "Lightening War." Hitler than turned his armies West. In the Lightening War he took all of Western Europe, culminating in his conquest of Paris. In North Africa the tide turned against the British and on June 20th the German General Erwin Rommel waged a final attack and won. Now there was nothing to prevent him from pushing all the way to Egypt; and after Egypt there was nothing between him and the defenseless homeland. In the face of all of this, somewhere within the ethnic fiber of this phenomenal bloodline, there was the persistence of this song of life and hope.

"Yea, though I walk through the valley of the shadow of death, I will fear no evil for thou art with me; thy rod and thy staff they comfort me. Thou preparest a table before me in the presence of mine enemies:"

Psalm 23:4-5 KJV

Chapter 15

Fear – The Great Disabler

"Behold, I am the Lord, the God of all flesh: is there any thing too hard for me?"

Jeremiah 32:27 KJV

Through Jeremiah, we find God's making an open declaration that when it comes to Him, nothing falls beyond the realm of possibilities. No matter how great the turbulence might be around those who embrace His presence, and accept His divine sovereignty, He always has and always will be a bridge over troubled waters. It is clear in this scripture that God is directly challenging the spirit of doubt. God's strategy here is to disable the great disabler – fear. I say great because of the number of lives this spirit has claimed and the number of casualties it has produced.

In the previous chapter we shared how by all accounts, the Jews had suffered a tremendous defeat and rout throughout all of Europe. Hitler had now set his sights on driving the final nail in their coffin as a people, by denying them their right to exist even in their Jewish homeland. And so the Jews in Palestine were prepared to offer maximum resistance. The Haganah or young Jews would engage in guerilla warfare against the Germans. This new Israeli generation of Palestine longed to fight the Nazi under its own flag. The prevailing question was, would those who sat idly by including the Church, and watched in silence the merciless slaughter of six million Jews, be prepared to lend their support to this noble effort? It was understandable why the Jews saw the Nazis as their most hated enemies, and why the Arabs generally supported them. To the Arabs there was sound logic to their thinking. Anwar Sadat put it this way, "Germany is the enemy of our enemy England, so the enemy of our enemy is our friend." It has been said that all evil needs to succeed is for good people to do nothing.

Therefore, the Church can not afford to allow the mistakes of the past to be repeated. There must be a strong identifiable presence that is recognized by the Church globally. One that is profoundly accepted as the original order set by God Himself. In order for this to happen we must be prepared to disable the great disabler, fear.

"And the Lord God called unto Adam, and said unto him, Where art thou? And he said, I heard thy voice in the garden, and I was afraid, because I was naked; and I hid myself.
Genesis 3:9-10 KJV

Adam feared God in that he felt naked and alone. That is what fear does. It separates us not only from God, but also in many cases from each other. We have all been reared in a world plagued with human suffering and death. We develop fear that is born out of uncertainty, and grieve in our hearts because we were never built to handle loss. So we strive to avoid any circumstance that will create fear in an attempt to control pain. Sometimes fear can be a good thing, but oftentimes those things which we shy away or try to hide from, are the very things that are needed to bring us to a required or desired place. God is calling us to a collective effort. He is calling us to a corporate move. The one thing we can not do, is to be so afraid that we are not willing to embrace the mission that has been clearly set before us.

In 1944 Winston Churchill ordered the formation of a Jewish Brigade group. In 1945 the Jewish Brigade joined troops from the United States, Britain and five other allied countries. On May 5, 1945, Churchill announced that hostilities would officially end one minute after midnight. For the Western allies it was a time of rejoicing, for though they had sacrificed one million of their people, they had won the victory and now they could look forward to a brighter future.

For the Jews it was different. The end of the war was only the lifting of the veil that disguised their agony. It was the lowest period in all of their long history. The effects of the Holocaust were now visible and the spectacle went beyond their greatest apprehensions. With all they had suffered and all they had accomplished, once again the feelings of anxiety, agitation caused by the presence or nearness of death or injury, gripped their hearts. Fear can disable and cripple you. It can also cause you to be torn apart to the point where you can't function, or respond to clear and present danger. However, the Jews of Palestine could not afford the luxury of this kind of condition no more than we can today.

In 1945 with wars end, the British labor party with a favorable immigration policy in Palestine was swept into power. A new cabinet was formed, but their liberal policies were challenged by the Arab states which stated that there was simply no more room in Palestine for Jewish immigrants. One and a half million Jews were all that remained from pre-war Europe's eight million. They had been left to endure starvation and bitter cold without any clear end in sight. The Jews that had kept their lives had kept little else except a hope of escape from the scenes of their torment. Yet through extraordinary perseverance, and shear determination as though being driven by some unforeseen force, the Jews finally got their day in court.

In 1948 a resolution was adopted that Palestine would become a Jewish State. The Arab nations objected vigorously with blood and fire. Forty-five million Arabs against 350 thousand Jews, but still the Jewish group prevailed. May 14, 1948 was the day of Israel's birth. A Jewish State was proclaimed in Palestine which would forever be known as the State of Israel. Israel endured the onslaught of the Arab Nations and on May 14, 1948 the United States recognized the Israeli government as a Sovereign Nation. Jewish exile had ended among cheers, gunfire and blood. On that date the State of Israel knew the fear of death and the taste of birth at the same moment. By 1967 the waters were troubled again by what was to be called the Six

Day War. The Soviet Union had issued false reports to Egypt that Israel was planning an attack on Syria. Once again the hand of God was being forced by Israel's enemies. Egyptian troops moved into Sinai after the removal of United Nations forces. A blockade was set up denying Israel access to Persian Gulf oil. This was a blatant act of war. Arabs in Saudi Arabia had now pledged forces for the battle. Now the Egyptian president would declare that "our goal is to destroy Israel." Arabs everywhere were encouraged to join the "Jihad," the holy war against Israel. With Syria north, Egypt west, Saudi Arabia and Jordan to the south, people all over the world feared the death and total destruction of Israel. A blood battle ensued, but in six days Israel went from serious danger to successful resistance. For the first time in a great number of years Israel now controlled territories four times it's previous size, land that she had never dreamed of possessing.

Now what else could have caused this kind of a victory except the providential hand of God? The unbelievable had happened, after years of absence Israel had returned to the heart of Jerusalem. In the newly enlarged land of Israel, Israelis' rediscovered sites intimately connected to the history of the Bible. The most dramatic achievement of the Six Day War was the return of old Jerusalem and the Western wall of the Temple Mount - the symbolic center of the Jewish faith. What an amazing move of God, the same God who said to Joshua be not afraid, as I was with Moses, so shall I be with you. We know that to some the idea of re-establishing the Jerusalem Council sounds absurd, and that it is like trying to recover that which has already fallen, or replacing that which is irreplaceable. But our God is the righteous judge and even though an unrighteous judgment has been rendered, and the sentence of failure has been announced, it does not prove itself against the mind and plan of the Great I Am. For God's word and our belief and faith in that word, has the strength to disable the great disabler.

"For God hath not given us the spirit of fear; but of power, and of love, and of sound mind."

2 Timothy 1:7 KJV

Chapter 16

The Re-Covering of the Church

"And there shall come forth a rod out of the stem of Jesse, and a branch shall grow out of his roots: and the spirit of the Lord shall rest upon him, the spirit of wisdom and understanding, the spirit of counsel and might, the spirit of knowledge and the fear of the Lord;"

Isaiah 11:1-2 KJV

"I am the vine, ye are the branches. He that abideth in me, and I in him, the same bringeth forth much fruit of itself, for without me ye can do nothing."

John 15:5 KJV

In his prophecy, Isaiah informs us that from the bloodline of Jesse would come a rod (King David) and from the roots of that rod, a branch which was Jesus. Some 700 years later, in the New Testament Book of John, we are made witnesses to an extraordinary transfer or handoff. All of the attributes that the Spirit of God had given or set upon Jesus, He now gives, or sets upon His Church which was headed by His Disciples. "He that abideth in me, and I in him, the same bringeth forth much fruit of itself."

We are clearly in the season of Isaiah's prophecy, which was revisited by Jesus in John Chapter 15. Although many of the events of the prophecy have yet to take place, it is certain that the stage is set and the curtain is going up. As Isaiah speaks directly to what we have been proposing all along. The spirit of counsel and might are two terms that cannot be misunderstood. To counsel is to instruct, guide and direct from a position of knowledge and authority. Might is power, influence, rule and strength. These would be the general workings and characteristics of the Jerusalem Council.

And it shall make him of quick understanding in the fear of the Lord: and he shall not judge after the sight of his eyes, neither reprove after the hearing of his ears."

Isaiah 11:3 KJV

The scripture goes on to say that the branch shall trust in the judgments received from God. "Understanding in the fear of the Lord," and that He (the branch) shall not be dictated to or influenced by outside forces or circumstances. The inner workings of the Council shall be governed by its members being led by the spirit of God; they shall set the precepts and ordinances concerning themselves. They shall also be chosen from an assembly of Jewish believers in the Gospel of Christ who have their residence in Jerusalem. In the hearts of these men, and of their own admission, they should be in total agreement with the embodiment of Jesus' prayer.

"That they all may be one; as thou, Father, art in me, and I in thee, that they also may be one in us: that the world may believe that thou hast sent me."
John 17:21 KJV

Just as the Supreme Court of the United States, the Jerusalem Council members should hold a lifetime seat. For this reason their character should be assessed among their peers.

"And it shall come to pass in that day, that the Lord shall set his hand again the second time to recover the remnant of his people, which shall be left, from Assyria, and from Egypt, and from Pathos, and from Cush, and from Elam, and from Shinar, and from Hamath, and from the islands of the sea."
Isaiah 11:11 KJV

The first time God set His hand upon Israel was a physical recovery of her back to the Holy Land in 1948; it was then that she was recognized by the world as a Sovereign Nation. However, the second recovery will be a spiritual one that will be inaugurated by the Church, which has been identified in scripture as the branch of the vine or stem of Jesse. The duties of the branch or council must include, but are not limited to:

- *Speaking out against anti-Semitism globally;*
- *Declaring genocide as an ungodly act that should not be tolerated by existing world powers - no people should have to experience another Holocaust;*
- *Provide delegates to attend world conferences and the United Nations assemblies;*
- *In the spirit of celebration, to set times and agendas for holy week festivals around the world, taking into consideration the location and resources of those who make up the Church. Whether its waving huge colorful banners, being accompanied by dancing and music or waving a twig and throwing sand in the air, all of it will represent the oneness that God has called us to;*
- *Periodically directives should be issued to the body, admonishing it towards the great commission and to continue in its own holy war against all that seeks to defy the Church's "Rights of Passage." These directives should be accompanied by blessings, prophecy and words of wisdom, all received under the anointing of the Holy Spirit.*

"For the time is come that judgment must begin at the house of God: and if it first begin at us, what shall the end be of them that obey not the gospel of God?

1 Peter 4:17 KJV

As we move forward, the Church's competitive spirit within its own ranks has to die. It is imperative that we strive to show organizational unity. To be successful we must be prepared to operate on multiple fronts to include literature, politics and the arts; to speak boldly against those who threaten Israel. We know that any threat that is being leveled against the Jewish people is also being leveled against the Church.

There are many who say they support Israel's right to live peaceably as a Sovereign Nation in the God given ancient home of their fathers. Yet, whenever Israel tries to defend that right the outcry against her is immediate. The anti-Israel protest in the Arab world and Europe are massive and loud. Even in the streets of American cities protestors have called for Israel to be nuked and the Jews to be gassed. At the same time the large majority of American Christians who say they support Israel's right of self-defense are most often silent. For this reason there must be an outpouring of support for the removal both spiritually and practically, of the Church from Rome back to the heart of Jerusalem. The Jerusalem Council must be recognized as the resurrected portion of a disassembled body – the Church.

"They are all gone out of the way, they are together become unprofitable; there is none that doeth good, no, not one."
Romans 3:12 KJV

There are certain advantages connected with being the center of the Church that Jerusalem has yet to enjoy; not only in the way of financial contributions, but also by having a global voice always at the ready to cry out in her behalf. That is why our people must be educated to the nature of the warfare that is currently being waged against the Judeo-Christian Community. We must be prepared to constantly confront organizations such as Neo-Nazis, the Aryan brotherhood and radical Islam. Those who work diligently to ensure that everything that Israel does will come across as a negative. The most concerning of these groups is radical Islam. Brigitte Gabriel, founder of American Congress for Truth says, "Hamas has the largest infrastructure of all terrorist organizations on American soil today."

We have been infiltrated by people who want the Koran to replace the Constitution, the Torah and the Bible. "They (Radical Islam) are not trying to imitate our way of life - they are not interested in becoming a part of our culture, they are here with an agenda to make Islam the law of the land" says Nonie Darwish, who is an outspoken advocate for progress, minority rights, human and women's rights in the Middle East and the author of *"Now They Call Me Infidel: Why I Renounced Jihad for America, Is-*

rael and the War on Terror." They believe strongly that through guerrilla warfare and clever covert maneuvers, they will one day march on the White House, and that the domination of Islam and its ideas, with God's help will turn the White House into their house. Some view the situation in the Middle East between radical Islam and Israel as a clash of cultures, but the bombings and missile attacks are actually part of a campaign of Jihad, the holy war, to bring down the West and to undermine the very foundation of Christianity and Judaism. These are the same people who killed 100 thousand Algerians, fellow Muslims who disagreed with their branch of Islam. Now I must emphasize that this kind of behavior does not come from all Muslims or Islamic Muslims. Most are God fearing and peace loving people and they must be supported and applauded as such. However, ten to fifteen percent of 1.4 billion people are still a lot of folk who see you as a living target that must be destroyed.

In essence, one can say that Islam has been hijacked by Hamas; that particular strand that challenges the sacredness of life. We must make note of the fact that the propaganda of radical Islam is the same as Nazi Germany, the same hate speech, the same paranoia and us against them. Christian Churches in many places such as Bosnia, Indonesia, Bagdad and the Philippines, to name a few, have been repeatedly bombed and destroyed.

In the 1930's the danger of Nazism was there in everything that Hitler said, wrote and did. In the corruption of German youth, through propaganda a whole generation as early as grammar school, was swept into Hitler's program of anti-Semitism. People thought then that this was a German problem, a limited disagreement to be worked out between Germans and Jews. They could not connect the dots or the acts together. Islamic fundamentalism is a global network and a genuine threat to all that Christianity and Judaism represents. We know that history has a way of repeating itself, but this time that is something we can not allow. It is so important that the Christian community under-stand fully how serious it is for the Church, the people of Israel, and the Nations of the world in general, to reestablish the Jeru-salem Counsel. How can we build on the Judeo-Christian values that are essential to world peace and progress, if its foundation is not in place? It's like children who have been left alone while their parents went off to attend to other chores. Needless to say, the children had a ball rearranging the house by turning it into a virtual playground. But as the clock on the wall signaled the soon return of the parent, the children got busy in a hasty attempt to put everything back in order, so that when the parent re-entered the house they would find everything in its proper place. We are not about the business of pointing fingers and certainly not at the Catholic Church, because all of us are aware of the great work this Church has done throughout the world.

The imprint of their mission to care for the sick, to feed, house and educate the less fortunate people of many nations, can hardly be ignored. Surely God will smile on the benevolent contributions that they have made to much of mankind. That being said however, we must be willing to reflect on and make note of some historical facts. During the middle ages most peo-ple assumed that the Holy Roman Empire was God's kingdom on earth. This lifted their laws and aspirations for world domi-nance above God. It was this ideology coupled with a gross misinterpretation of God's word that led to so much violence and bloodshed during that same period.

"And in the days of these kings shall the God of heaven set up a kingdom which shall never be destroyed: and the kingdom shall not be left to other people, but it shall break in pieces and consume all these kingdoms, and it shall stand for ever".
Daniel 2:44 KJV

While the old Roman Empire still existed, most Jews and Christians believed that it would be the fourth and final kingdom that Daniel prophesied about. Many falsely assumed therefore, that the antichrist would emerge on the world scene once the Roman Empire had expired. The Germans more than any other people, felt it their divine duty to preserve this Holy Roman Empire so that the antichrist might not appear. Time and again, whenever the Empire was threatened to be extinguished it would somehow, muster enough strength to raise itself once more. This was usually behind one powerful leader supported by a powerful religious head in Rome. If we are to rely on and follow prophecy, then we must follow it to its completion. What the people of these Empires failed to understand, was that these same Roman resurrections were also prophesied in the Bible. Its true that the Bible does prophecy of four world ruling Empires, but the final Empire after it was crushed in 476 A.D., was to be resurrected ten more times; the last seven of which would be in conjunction with the papal authority in Rome as the resurrected "Holy Roman Empire".

Adolf Hitler believed that the senseless murders of millions of Jews was God inspired, which is the same ideology shared by radical Islam. In the 1930's the Grand Mufti of Jerusalem, the leader of the Arab National Movement and one of the founders of radical Islam, was invited to Germany by Hitler who befriended him saying, "We have the same goal, the extermination of the Jews." From that point on radical Islam would follow the precepts and carry out the strategies of Nazi Germany to the letter.

"And the Lord said unto Cain, where is Abel thy brother? And he said, I know not: Am I my brother's keeper? And He said, what has thou done? The voice of thy brother's blood crieth unto me from the ground."

Genesis 4:9-10 KJV

Based on the previous scripture, we are now making an earnest appeal to those who are leaders of the Roman Catholic

Church movement, to hear the cries of the blood stained past by not only denouncing the anti-Semitic raging of radical Islam, but also expressing their support and offering their blessings to the Jerusalem Council, and the removal of the Center and Head of the Church from Rome back to the heart of Jerusalem. We all know that it is totally irrational to ask or even expect the recovery of the Church, and the quest for world peace to rest on the shoulders of one man.

"For the love of Christ constraineth us; because we thus judge, that if one died for all, then were all dead: and that he died for all, that they which live should not henceforth live unto themselves, but unto him which died for them, and rose again. Therefore henceforth know we no man after the flesh: yea, though we have known Christ after the flesh, yet now henceforth know we him no more."

2 Corinthians 5:14-16 KJV

And so it is written, that this marshalling of the household of faith will not require the official seal of approval of any man or group of men. We must simply redirect our prayers and reaffirm our blood ties with Israel, offering our total resolution to stand with and labor in behalf of the Jerusalem Council.

"But Israel shall be saved in the LORD with an everlasting salvation: ye shall not be ashamed nor confounded world without end. For thus saith the LORD that created the heavens; God himself that formed the earth and made it; he hath established it, he created it not in vain, he formed it to be inhabited: I am the LORD; and there is none else. I have not spoken in secret, in a dark place of the earth: I said not unto the seed of Jacob, Seek ye me in vain: I the LORD speak righteousness, I declare things that are right. Assemble yourselves and come; draw near together, ye that are escaped of the nations: they have no knowledge that set up the wood of their graven image, and pray unto a god that cannot save."

Isaiah 45:17-20 KJV

When we are asked *just how we intend to do this thing,* there is but one answer we can give; we are simply acknowledging a fact and reaffirming its truth...

the Jerusalem Council was already set in place, and sanctioned by God over 2000 years ago.

Conclusion

It is imperative that we understand for the first time in our generation, that every prayer set before God has an exceptional possibility of being answered. We are definitely living in a season of recovery, and the re-establishment of the Jerusalem Council in Jerusalem is part of that recovery process.

For years we have grappled with the question; why have we not shared the abundant blessings, and miracles of the first Church as many of our Judeo-Christian leaders have promised? The answer is now before us, we must first return to God's pattern and design to recreate the "blessing zone." Our God is a God of atmosphere, who dwells in the midst of His people and their praises. We have learned that atmosphere fosters or advances attitudes, and attitudes have much to say about how we conduct business.

"Be kindly affectioned one to another with brotherly love; in honour preferring one another; Not slothful in business; fervent in spirit; serving the Lord;"
Romans 12:10-11 KJV

As for the Church we cannot afford to go on with business as usual, that's why all members of the Universal Judeo-Christian assembly are being asked to publicly declare before God, family, friends and neighbors; that they will be praying for and lending support to, the reestablishment of a Jewish-Christian Council in Jerusalem. We are honored by the prospect that God has chosen us to bear witness to and partner with the most exciting, electrifying and inspirational movement of our time. The Apostle James has taught us that faith without works is dead. Although this is truly the season of harvest and recovery, there will be no harvest without sowing. We would only be putting ourselves in a position where our words appear to be nothing more than empty rhetoric. We therefore request all who have read and understand this Clarion Call for action to contact us at:

Chosen Generation
Post Office Box 326 - Clinton, Maryland 20735
Office: (301) 248-4834
chosen.generation@live.com

"For as the body without the spirit is dead, so faith without works is dead also, being alone."

James 2:26 KJV

Biography

Bishop Royce L. Woods is the Senior Pastor of Holy Trinity Worship Center International, located in Washington, DC. Born in Raleigh, NC, he is the 17th of 18 children born to the late Bishop John and Mary Woods. At an early age, his family moved from Raleigh to Washington, DC.

After serving four years in the United States Navy where he received the Vietnam Campaign Medal and an Honorable Discharge. Bishop Woods began his ministry on the streets of the Nation's Capitol. His work has taken him across the country where he has forged strong relationships with both Jew and Gentile Christians. The last twenty plus years has been spent building community-based training and outreach programs through the development of the Chosen Generation, which provides and creates hands-on opportunities for concerned business and government officials to make a difference in their communities.

He holds a Bachelor in Biblical Studies, Masters in Divinity, Masters in Christian Psychology and Pastoral Counseling, and a Doctorate in Theology.

He lives in Prince Georges County, Maryland with his wife Catherine.

Bishop Woods is without a doubt a man on a mission for Christ. He gains strength from his most quoted scripture Romans 8:31; "What shall we say to these things? If God be for us, who can be against us?"

Bibliography

Anderson, Claud. *Black Labor, White Wealth: The Search for Power and Economic Justice.* Edgewood, Maryland, U.S.A.:: Duncan & Duncan, 1994.

Eban, Abba. *My People: The Story of the Jews.* New York: Random House, 1968.

Gilbert, Martin. *The Holocaust: A History of the Jews of Europe During the Second World War.* New York: First Owl Books, 1987.

Goll, James W. *Coming Israel Awakening, The: Gazing into the Future of the Jewish People and the Church.* Grand Rapids, MI: Chosen Books, 2009.

Harpur, James, and Marcus Braybrooke. *The Collegeville Atlas of the Bible.* Collegeville, MN: Liturgical Press, 1999.

Peterson, Eugene H. *The Message: The Bible in Contemporary Language.* Colorado Springs, CO: Navpress Publishing Group, 2005.

Roth, Sid. *The Race To Save The World: CHRISTIANS AND JEWS MUST UNITE TO FORM THE ONE NEW MAN.* New York: Charisma House, 2004.

Scripture quotations marked KJV are from the King James Version of the Bible.